ESSAYS IN INTERNATIONAL ECONOMICS

No. 226, February 2002

THE EVOLVING ASIAN FINANCIAL ARCHITECTURE

GRAHAM BIRD

AND

RAMKISHEN S. RAJAN

INTERNATIONAL ECONOMICS SECTION

DEPARTMENT OF ECONOMICS
PRINCETON UNIVERSITY
PRINCETON, NEW JERSEY

INTERNATIONAL ECONOMICS SECTION
EDITORIAL STAFF

Gene M. Grossman *Director*
Pierre-Olivier Gourinchas *Assistant Director*
Margaret B. Riccardi, *Editor*
Sharon B. Ernst, *Editorial Aide*
Lalitha H. Chandra, *Subscriptions and Orders*

Library of Congress Cataloging-in-Publication Data

Bird, Graham
    The evolving Asian financial architecture / Graham Bird and Ramkishen S. Rajan .
    p. cm. — (Essays in international economics ; no. 226)
    Includes bibliographical references.
    ISBN 0-88165-133-8
    1. Finance—Asia. 2. Financial crises—Asia. I. Rajan, Ramkishen S. II. Title. III.
Essays in international economics (Princeton, N.J.); no. 226.

HG187.A2 B57 2002   2002019154
332'.095—dc21   CIP

Printed in the United States of America by Princeton University Printing Services at Princeton, New Jersey

International Standard Serial Number: 0071-142X
International Standard Book Number: 0-88165-133-8
Library of Congress Catalog Card Number: 2002019154

International Economics Section
  Department of Economics, Fisher Hall
  Princeton University
  Princeton, New Jersey 08544-1021

Tel: 609-258-4048
Fax: 609-258-1374
E-mail: ies@princeton.edu
Url: www.princeton.edu/~ies

CONTENTS

TABLES

FIGURES

THE EVOLVING ASIAN FINANCIAL ARCHITECTURE

1 Introduction

The debate about reforming the international financial architecture began in the mid-1990s in the aftermath of the 1994 Mexican peso crisis. It was the East Asian crisis of 1997–98, however, that breathed life into the debate and helped to shape it. The discussion has subsequently centered on trying to prevent crises from happening and on dealing with them effectively and efficiently when they do. In addressing these central issues, the debate has ranged over many topics, including domestic financial reform, debt and crisis management, exchange-rate policy, and the role of the International Monetary Fund (IMF).

Viewed from a political-economy perspective, it was always unlikely that the debate would lead to a fundamental reform of the world's monetary system. After all, according to most conventional indicators, the global economy was performing quite well in the second half of the 1990s, so why was reform needed? Contagion turned out to be much more of a regional than a global phenomenon, and, in any case, there was no clear consensus about what changes should be made to the financing and adjustment mechanisms that define the international monetary system. Of course, modest changes have been made, but it is difficult to describe these as altering the international financial architecture.

Nevertheless, although reform at the global level has been piecemeal and slow and is likely to remain so, there may be more potential for reform at the regional level. The crisis of 1997–98 imposed severe economic costs on the Asian economies and, in some cases, also social and political costs. Because the strength and sustainability of recovery from the crisis still remains in some doubt, there may well be some motivation for reform (Park, 2001b).

This essay examines key aspects of a new Asian financial architecture. It describes and evaluates progress, identifies the issues that must still be resolved, and addresses the prospects for future reform. In particular, it asks three questions. First, to what extent have the domestic

The authors are grateful for useful comments and suggestions on an earlier draft of this essay by Richard Pomfret and by an anonymous referee. The usual disclaimer applies.

1

financial deficiencies that contributed to the crisis in 1997–98 been put right, and have domestic financial and corporate systems been strengthened adequately? Second, what are the lessons for exchange-rate policy in the region? Did the fixation with pegged exchange rates help to cause the crisis, and if so, does this imply that the Asian economies should opt either for firm fixity in the form of a common regional currency or for flexible exchange rates? Third, in providing short-term liquidity in the midst of a crisis, is there a role for regional arrangements? Could this lead to the establishment of an Asian monetary fund (AMF), and if so, what would be the division of labor between such a fund and the IMF?

In what follows, we attempt to work through each of these questions. To anticipate a little, our broad conclusion is that there is significantly more scope for a new *Asian* financial architecture than for a new *international* financial architecture, and, indeed, there are signs of evolution in this direction. There are also, however, potential pitfalls that should be avoided. Appropriately designed and implemented, a new Asian financial architecture does not threaten multilateral reform; on the contrary, it may support and protect the world's financial system.

2 The Debate About a New Financial Architecture

Reforming the International Financial Architecture

According to some observers, the debate about a new international financial architecture was launched at the G-7 Halifax summit in 1995 and concluded at the Cologne summit in 1999 (Kenen, 2001). Like many initially appealing and catchy phrases, the "international financial architecture" has, at best, been only vaguely defined, with contributors to the debate laying the emphasis in different places. Broadly speaking, however, the topics covered have included the provision of economic and financial information, domestic financial supervision and regulation, liability management, crisis lending and management, and reform of the international financial institutions, particularly the IMF (Table 1). The background to the debate was set by the Mexican peso crisis in 1994. This had demonstrated, if demonstration were needed, that international capital was now highly mobile and that capital volatility— both sudden inflows and sudden outflows of capital—could cause severe economic problems. Even before the architecture debate really got going, therefore, the Bretton Woods Commission and others had spent time discussing ways of dealing with capital volatility and the potential need for larger amounts of emergency lending. It was the

2

TABLE 1

COMPONENTS CONSTITUTING REFORM OF THE INTERNATIONAL
FINANCIAL ARCHITECTURE

I. *Detecting and Monitoring External Vulnerability*: Although good macroeconomic policies and adequate foreign reserves remain the key to reducing vulnerability, work has concentrated on improving IMF surveillance of policies and on tools to help countries better assess the risks they face.

II. *Strengthening Financial Systems*: Financial regulators need to upgrade the supervision of banks and other financial institutions to keep up with the modern global economy and ensure that risk management and other practices keep institutions from getting into difficulties.

III. *International Standards and Codes*: Adherence to international standards and codes of good practice helps ensure that economies function well at the national level, which is a key prerequisite for a well-functioning international system.

IV. *Capital-Account Issues*: Architecture reform aims to help countries benefit from international capital flows, an important element of which is helping them open to such flows in ways that avoid risks and emphasize careful preparation.

V. *Sustainable Exchange-Rate Regimes*: Financial crises have often been marked by inconsistencies between the exchange-rate regime and other economic policies. The IMF is advising countries to choose a regime that fits its needs, especially in light of the risks of pegged exchange rates for countries open to international capital flows.

VI. *Involving the Private Sector in Forestalling and Resolving Crises*: Better involvement of the private sector in crisis prevention and management can limit moral hazard, strengthen market discipline by fostering better risk assessment, and improve the prospects for both debtors and creditors.

VII. *Reform of IMF Financial Facilities and Related Issues*: The IMF is implementing important changes to help focus its lending on crisis prevention and to ensure the more effective use of IMF funds.

VIII. *Measures to Increase Transparency*: Measures are being taken to make available timely, reliable data, plus information about economic policies and practices, to inform both policymakers and market participants, and to reduce the risk of crisis.

SOURCE: Adapted from IMF (2001b, p. 1).

East Asian crisis in 1997, however, that subsequently moved the architecture debate forward.

Why had neither the Mexican nor the Asian crisis been widely anticipated? What had caused them, and had they been well handled? It was in the context of these questions that attention began to focus on the availability of adequate information. Perhaps, for example, prediction had been poor because the extent of forward commitments in foreign-exchange markets had sometimes not been appreciated, making the adequacy of international reserves rather less than appeared, or because fiscal deficits had been inappropriately measured. Moreover, although commentators differed about the degree to which the crises were caused by illiquidity as opposed to deficient fundamentals, and indeed about what constituted "fundamentals," few departed from the view that weak domestic financial systems had something to do with the problem. In its most extreme form, inadequate risk analysis was presented as a dimension of crony capitalism. On this basis, the reform of domestic financial systems was presented as a critical step toward strengthening the international financial system. The architecture debate also reinforced what appeared to have been overlooked principles about liquidity mismatches and foreign-exchange risk. The dangers of borrowing short and lending long, as well as the dangers of carrying unhedged foreign-currency liabilities (and the resulting vulnerability) were, again, featured prominently in the discussion.

The architecture debate acknowledged that even with improved information and superior risk analysis and liability management, not all crises would be avoided. Another crucial element in the discussions, therefore, related to the handling of crises once they occurred and the roles that private capital markets and international financial institutions would play. What could be done to "bail in" private creditors and to avoid a rush for the exits? Should bond contracts be redesigned to include collective-action clauses? Should the IMF endorse standstills on external-debt repayments? Or should the IMF become a more fully fledged international lender of last resort (see Jeanne and Wyplosz, 2001; Willett, 2001a; and references cited therein) Should it, furthermore, modify its conditionality? These issues and many more were part of the architecture debate.

Progress To Date: Unfinished Business

But what was the debate ever likely to achieve? And if it has now been concluded, what has it achieved? History suggests that discrete and fundamental reform of the international financial system is an unlikely event. It occurred in 1944 at Bretton Woods under quite special circumstances, and it occurred in 1973 with the collapse of the Bretton Woods system. In the latter case, however, the reform was less the outcome of a debate about the design of the system and more a matter

4

of expediency; pegging exchange rates had not worked, so there was little alternative to flexible rates. The Committee of Twenty (C-20) did indeed "debate" the design of the international financial system in the early 1970s but achieved relatively little of significance. The 1990s debate about the international financial architecture shares much more with the C-20 episode than it does with the earlier Bretton Woods debate; its achievements have been modest and are likely to remain so.

For fundamental reform to occur, a number of criteria must be met. There has to be broad agreement that existing arrangements are not working satisfactorily, and this agreement must include those countries that wield the greatest power in decisionmaking. Moreover, there has to be a similar consensus about the nature of needed reform. In the latter part of the 1990s, economic performance in many of the world's largest and most influential economies was relatively strong when judged in terms of economic growth, unemployment, and inflation (although Japan was a notable exception). Moreover, in terms of the U.S. dollar, the Japanese yen, and the euro, there is little to challenge the superiority of flexible exchange rates. There was the possibility in the mid-1990s that further financial crises could plunge the world into recession, but this threat did not materialize. Although crises continued to occur in East Asia, Russia, Brazil, Turkey, and Argentina, these tended to be regional affairs from which the United States and Europe remained relatively insulated. There is, in any case, a catch-22 in the link between economic crises and reform. Without a crisis, why is reform needed? In the midst of a crisis, however, there is insufficient time to pursue fundamental reform, and "band-aid" reform is much more likely. Assuming the crisis passes, it again becomes more difficult to justify fundamental reform; after all the band-aid will appear to have done its job.

In large measure, this is the sequence that occurred in the aftermath of the financial crises in Mexico and East Asia. International liquidity was injected in a somewhat *ad hoc* fashion. The world avoided large-scale contagion. The crises passed, and the momentum for reform—as much as it existed—was lost. What has emerged is much more an attempt to formalize *"ad hoccery."*

Having discovered, after the event, that information was inadequate, the IMF has sought to enhance transparency by collecting and disseminating more information through its General and Special Data Dissemination Standards and its Policy Framework Papers. The Basle Committee has continued to fine-tune its guidelines for capital adequacy and prudential supervision and regulation, and the IMF has introduced

5

Contingent Credit Lines (CCLs) to provide precautionary resources in the event of contagion from a crisis. But although the logic behind these reforms may be sound, they hardly constitute a new international financial architecture. There can be little guarantee that all relevant information is now being collected and even less that it will always be accurately interpreted. Guidelines on good practice in terms of domestic financial supervision are only helpful if implemented, but there are few structured incentives to put them in place. For its part, the CCL has been heavily criticized and remains unused.

The IMF has undertaken a number of internal reviews covering the range of its lending facilities, conditionality, and quotas, but it is difficult, at present, to pick out any changes that have been much more than cosmetic. For example, abandoning the Buffer Stock Financing Facility, which had not been used for fifteen years, and rescinding the contingency component of the Compensatory and Contingency Financing Facility, which had not be used for eight years, represent housecleaning, rather than a new architecture. Add to this little progress on the redesign of bond contracts and on debt standstills, and it remains difficult to be upbeat about the achievements of the architecture debate. Issues have been aired, and modest and piecemeal modifications have been made, but a new architecture, hardly![1]

Is this situation likely to change? Perhaps it is overambitious to expect rapid reform. Clearly, a global depression of 1930s' proportions could recreate some of the circumstances that allowed success at Bretton Woods in 1944, although the unanimity of views relating to what is wrong and what needs to be done might not be so easily replicated.[2] In reality, the continuing pivotal role of the U.S. dollar, along with the often apparently inexhaustible supply of liquidity with which the United States can finance its current-account balance-of-payments deficit, rules out the United States as a leading advocate of

---

[1] This said, it is true that the internal debate about reforming the IMF and its policies is clearly not over. For example, the new deputy managing director of the IMF, Anne Krueger, has proposed the establishment of an international bankruptcy arrangement by which a country facing a possible crisis in confidence can restructure unsustainable debts in an orderly and timely manner. This system would enable the IMF to offer a crisis-hit debtor country temporary legal protection from creditors so as to restructure its debt obligations. Such an arrangement could prevent a similar problem from reoccurring and would be minimally disruptive in the short-term.

[2] According to Eichengreen and James (2001), one reason why international financial reforms are not occurring at a faster pace is that the recent financial crises do not appear to have threatened the global trading system.

fundamental reform. Similarly, the probability must be close to zero that any current member of the euro zone or of the European Union (EU), for that matter, will need to turn to the IMF for financial assistance. For the Europeans, reform at the regional level has largely replaced their direct interest in global financial reform, unless contagion from a crisis elsewhere, as for example in Russia, becomes, or threatens to become, a problem. The increasing indifference shown by the major economic powers to economic crises elsewhere in the world has been exemplified by the benign neglect shown by the United States with regard to the Argentine crisis in 2001–02. This posture seems unlikely to change in the near future.

The conclusion seems be that although there may be some scope for modest financial reform or redesign at the global level—the importance of which should not be understated—the possibility of establishing anything approaching a new international financial architecture is strictly limited. The very reasons that make a new architecture unlikely at the global level, however, may make it much more likely at the regional level.

The Asian Financial Architecture

It was mainly the Asian economies that suffered the costs of the 1997–98 crisis. These costs were substantial, representing shortfalls in output of up to 40 percent and significant declines in living standards. The costs linger, moreover, because with a recession of this size, even renewed economic growth will take some time to return an economy to its precrisis level. Although contagion at the global level was muted, the Asian crisis spread rapidly from Thailand to Korea, Indonesia, and other regional economies.[3] Even those that escaped the worst excesses of contagion were still adversely affected by negative changes in trade, interest rates, and exchange rates, let alone the effects of a pessimistic psychological bandwagon (Rajan, 2002c). Against this background, there may be relatively strong support within the region for reform that minimizes vulnerability to future crises and contagion. Even those countries in the region that managed to pass through the 1997–98 crisis reasonably unscathed may believe that they might subsequently not be so fortunate.

What about Japan, the regional hegemonic power? Unlike the United States, for which the 1990s were a decade of economic success, Japan seems to have been trapped in a low-level growth equilibrium. Indeed,

[3] "Korea" refers to the Republic of Korea (South Korea) throughout the essay.

the Japanese recovery that flickered in 1996 was hardly helped by the Asian crisis in the following two years (Rajan, 1998). Although the United States may appear to have been largely unconcerned by the crisis in Brazil in 1999 or the one in Argentina in 2001–02, it is reasonable to presume that Japan will be much more concerned about, and have a direct interest in avoiding, further economic crises in Asia (Chang and Rajan, 1999). There is always the possibility that inertia will set in as the 1997–98 crisis becomes a more distant memory, but this is more likely at the global level than at the regional level, where the full force of the crisis was experienced. Among the Asian economies, it seems there is both a much clearer picture of what was wrong with the situation that existed in 1997–98 and a broadly shared diagnosis of what needs to be put right.

This diagnosis contains a number of elements. First, weak domestic financial systems make economies vulnerable to crises. Weakness can result from inadequate risk analysis, maturity mismatches, and an inappropriate exchange-rate denomination of assets and liabilities. Second, pegging the value of a currency fairly firmly to the U.S. dollar may lead to economic and financial problems, irrespective of what currency-crisis model is adopted. When devaluation eventually occurs, its balance-sheet effects can rapidly transform a currency crisis into a domestic financial crisis, so that the devaluation itself has short-run recessionary effects. Third, once international reserves have been depleted to some threshold level, and in the absence of sufficient private-capital inflows, there will be little choice but to turn to the IMF, unless measures to block capital outflows are envisaged. International reserves that are deemed adequate, or even more than adequate, before a crisis can rapidly disappear, so that reserve depletion offers little more than a very short-term response. In addition, reserve depletion that is unsterilized will have significant recessionary domestic monetary effects. Sterilization, however, will offset improvements in the current account of the balance of payments. Although the economic fundamentals in the region's economies may not have been entirely sound, problems of illiquidity contributed significantly to the dimensions of the 1997–98 crises.

This analysis implies that to minimize the risks of future crises and to mitigate the effects of crises, any reform must address these matters. Because these are the issues that have largely constituted the agenda of the architecture debate, it is not surprising that the discussion about a new international financial architecture has been greatly stimulated by the East Asian crisis. As the debate has formed, it has therefore focused

8

on the issues that were particularly apposite in the case of Asia. Yet, the nature and very title of the discussion suggest that the resolution of the problems associated with the East Asian crisis requires action at the international level. The argument in this essay is that significant reform at the global level is unlikely, and that reform at the regional level has a greater chance of success. This regional reform should cover *domestic financial systems, exchange-rate regimes,* and *regional liquidity arrangements.*

3   Financial Containment and Restructuring in Asia

What Has Been Done?

Financial-sector restructuring has been presented as an essential element in structural-adjustment programs in the East Asian economies (Lane et al., 1999). There are two broad phases in resolving financial-system distress: containment and restructuring.

The containment, or distress-resolution, phase occurs during the onset of a financial crisis, when there has been a loss of confidence in the financial system. The primary strategic consideration during this phase is to stabilize the financial system and to prevent a credit crunch and an economic slowdown, which then exacerbates financial difficulties. This usually involves providing large-scale liquidity support to financial institutions. The secondary aim is to limit losses. This may involve closures of unviable banks, mergers, or even nationalization. In order to prevent bank panics, the government may also issue guarantees on liabilities of existing banks.[4] As the Indonesian experience illustrates, a failure to "contain" may exacerbate financial turbulence and have potentially severe sociopolitical repercussions.[5] Empirical analysis by Honohan and Klingebiel (2000) reveals that unlimited

---

[4] There is an important practical issue of being able to decide between *illiquid but solvent* and *insolvent* financial institutions. As noted by Lindgren et al. (2000, p. 23), of the Thai debacle,

   the selection of nonviable institutions to be closed relied largely on liquidity indicators, such as borrowing from the central banks. . . . The liquidity triggers typically included the size of central bank credit as a multiple of bank capital. Only later, as more information became available either through special audits or the supervisory process, could solvency indicators be used as criteria for choosing nonviable institutions.

[5] Two problems faced by Indonesia in particular, but also by the other crisis-hit economies during the phase, were the acute loss of macroeconomic confidence following excessive monetary creation to provide liquidity to the distressed financial system and the sudden (and nontransparent) closure of insolvent financial institutions.

9

deposit guarantees, open-ended liquidity support, and repeated recapitalizations are among the factors that can significantly add to the fiscal costs of banking crisis and restructuring.[6]

Having been through the containment stage, the five East Asian economies worst affected by the 1997–98 crisis, Indonesia, Korea, Malaysia, the Philippines, and Thailand (henceforth referred to as the "Asia-5" economies), are now embarked on a process of rehabilitation and restructuring.[7] At the risk of generalizing, governments in the Asia-5 economies have attempted to restructure their financial systems by

- closing commercial banks and finance companies;
- merging some existing institutions and nationalizing others;
- permitting foreign investment in the financial sector;
- injecting public funds into recapitalized viable banks;
- putting in place systematic asset-resolution strategies.

Table 2 provides information about the measures taken by the Asia-5 economies to restructure their financial systems.

With regard to asset resolution, all the Asia-5 economies except Thailand have transferred nonperforming loans (NPLs) from banks to centralized asset-management companies (AMCs).[8] In Thailand, banks were initially left individually responsible for creating their own AMCs. The Thai government did establish the Financial Restructuring Authority (FRA) in October 1997 to review rehabilitation plans of the fifty-eight suspended finance companies and to oversee their liquidation (all but two were closed). An asset-management company was also set up centrally, but only as a buyer (or bidder) of last resort for the lowest quality assets in order to prevent a fire sale of assets of the fifty-six closed finance companies (Rajan, 2001).

By 1999, all the economies had made some headway in reducing NPLs (Table 3). Commercial-bank ratios of NPLs fell to less than 10 percent in Korea and Malaysia, in response partly to rapid economic

---

[6] Accordingly, they favor a "strict" approach to crisis resolution rather than an "accommodating" one.

[7] For detailed discussions of financial restructuring in the Asia-5 economies, see Claessens, Djankov, and Klingebiel (1999); Lindgren et al. (2000); Asian Development Bank ([ADB] 2000); Asian Development Bank–Asia Recovery Information Centre ([ADB-ARIC] 2000, 2001a); World Bank (2000a, 2000b); and Kawaii (2002). Park (2001b) provides an overall assessment of the financial and corporate restructuring in the East Asian economies.

[8] See Klingebiel (1999) for a detailed discussion of cross-country experiences with the use of AMCs in resolutions of banking crises.

TABLE 2
SUMMARY OF MEASURES TO ADDRESS THE FINANCIAL CRISIS IN EAST ASIA

Measures	Indonesia	Korea	Malaysia	Philip-pines	Thailand
Containment measures					
Liquidity support	Yes	Yes	Yes	Yes	Yes
Introduction of a blanket guarantee	Yes	Yes	Yes	No	Yes
Institutional measures					
Establishment of an overarching restructuring authority	Yes	Yes	Yes[a]	No	No
Establishment of a separate bank-restructuring authority	Yes	No	Yes	No	No
Establishment of a centralized asset-management corporation	Yes	Yes[b]	Yes	No	No[c]
Adoption of a special corporate-debt-restructuring framework	Yes	Yes	Yes	No	Yes
Operational autonomy of restructuring agencies	Limited	Yes	Yes	n.a.	n.a.
Restructuring measures					
Intervention in weak or insolvent financial institutions, including:	Yes	Yes	Yes	Yes	Yes
Mergers of weak institutions	Yes[d]	Yes	Yes	Yes	Yes[d]
Closures of insolvent institutions	Yes	Yes	Yes	Yes	Yes
Use of public funds to purchase nonperforming assets	Yes	Yes	Yes	No	No
Use of public funds to recapitalize institutions, including:	Yes	Yes	Yes	No	Yes
State intervention in banks	Yes	Yes	Yes	No	Yes
Elimination or dilution of current shareholder stakes of insolvent banks	Yes	Yes	Yes	Yes	Yes
Other measures					
Measures to encourage corporate restructuring	Yes	Yes	Yes	Yes	Yes
Steps to improve prudential supervision and regulation	Yes	Yes	Yes	Yes	Yes

[a] Malaysia formed a steering committee chaired by the central banks.

[b] The powers of the preexisting AMC were substantially increased.

[c] The FRA was established to liquidate fifty-six closed finance companies, and the AMC was meant to deal with residual FRA assets.

[d] A number of government-owned intervened institutions were merged.

SOURCE: Lindgren et al. (2000).

recovery (that is, banks have to some extent grown out of their problems). In Thailand, by contrast, NPLs remained high, at about 30 percent, perhaps reflecting the Thai government's preference for a

TABLE 3

NONPERFORMING LOAN RATIOS AND FISCAL COSTS OF RESTRUCTURING
IN EAST ASIA, 1997–1999

(*Percent*)

	Share of NPLs to Total Loans: Official Estimate			Share of NPLs to Total Loans: Unofficial Estimate	Fiscal Costs of restructuring as Share of GDP
	End 1997	End 1998	Sept 1999	Peak Level	
Indonesia	n.a.	n.a.	n.a.	60–85	58
Korea	n.a.	7.6	6.6	20–30	16
Malaysia	n.a.	18.9	17.8	20–30	10
Philippines	5.4	11.0	13.4	15–25	n.a.
Thailand	19.8	45.0	44.7	50–70	32

NOTES: NPLs are measured on a three-month basis. The unofficial estimate includes assets carved out for sale by the AMCs.
SOURCE: ADB (2000).

more market-oriented approach to financial restructuring. According to some estimates, however, between one-fifth and one-third of the NPLs in Thailand are "strategic," in the sense that borrowers, although able to repay, have been unwilling to do so, because legal recourse by creditors tends to be ineffective. Interestingly, Thailand has announced that a centralized AMC will be established to carve out the stubbornly high levels of NPLs from the state and private banks (ADB-ARIC, 2001a, 2001b; Park, 2001b).

What Still Needs to Be Done?

A report on the Asia-5 economies by the Asia Recovery Information Centre (ADB-ARIC, 2000, pp. 12–13) describes the events relating to the cleaning up of the banks' balance sheets by the AMCs in the following way:

During 2000, debt restructuring through . . . [AMCs] has made further progress in Korea and Malaysia, as well as Indonesia. . . . The Korea Asset Management Corporation (KAMCO) purchased more than 50 percent of the banking system's NPLs by July 2000 and had disposed of 40 percent of those it had acquired. Danaharta had acquired a little more than 40 percent of NPLs in the Malaysian banking system by August 2000, amounting to about 15 percent of the country's GDP. It is estimated that, as of June 2000, Danaharta had disposed of 61 percent of the NPLs under its jurisdic-

12

tion. In Indonesia, it is estimated that more than 75 percent of the total NPLs in the banking system, amounting to 60 percent of GDP, are now under [the Indonesian Bank Restructuring Agency's] IBRA's control. However, uncooperative and politically powerful debtors, and an inadequate legislative and regulatory environment have hampered the recovery of asset values in the country. As of June 2000, only 0.35 percent, representing corporate loans, of acquired NPLs has been disposed of by IBRA. . . . In Thailand, it was reported that almost all the loans of closed financial institutions acquired by the Financial Sector Restructuring Agency (FRA) had been disposed of by December 1999. No data on debt restructuring by commercial banks are available, but some banks are reportedly back to profitability.

Thus, although these transfers have helped to recapitalize banks and reduce NPLs, the disposal of assets by the AMCs has been rather slow. This slowness is attributable, at least partly, to the fact that the assets transferred to the AMCs are corporate assets, rather than real-estate assets, which are easier to restructure. Additional factors such as political influence and uncertainties, powerful debtors and lack of interested buyers, inadequate bankruptcy and foreclosure laws, and opacity in operations and processes, are cited as reasons for the slow asset disposal in the regional economies (ADB-ARIC, 2000, 2001a, 2001b).

Failure to address banking-sector problems adequately can be a severe impediment to corporate-debt resolution and restructuring. Indirect evidence of market concerns about a lack of progress in financial restructuring in the Asia-5 economies is captured by trends in the ratio of the financial stock index to the overall (general) stock market index (ADB-ARIC, 2000). This ratio has recovered to its precrisis level only in Malaysia. At the other extreme, it is only about one-fourth of its precrisis level in Indonesia, and it has recently deteriorated rapidly in the Philippines. The indices in Korea and Thailand are stuck at about one-half of their precrisis values. This pattern appears to suggest that, with the possible exception of Malaysia, there is continuing concern about the health of the financial systems in the Asia-5 economies.

Slow progress toward corporate-debt restructuring is the single biggest obstacle to improving banks' balance sheets and, consequently, to the availability of domestic credit, particularly to small and medium-sized enterprises.[9] Table 4 summarizes the progress of corporate restructuring in four of the five crisis-hit economies. By and large,

[9] Small and medium-sized economies have been especially hard hit by the credit crunch, particularly because many are in the nontradable sector. In Thailand, small firms and households account for half of the NPLs (ADB, 2000; World Bank, 2000a, 2000b).

TABLE 4

PROGRESS WITH CORPORATE RESTRUCTURING IN EAST ASIA, 1999:Q3

	Indonesia	Korea	Malaysia	Thailand
Out-of-court procedures				
All or majority of financial institutions signed accord	No	Yes	Yes	Yes
Formal process of arbitration exists, with deadlines	No	No	Yes	Yes
Provision of penalties for noncompliance	No	Yes	No	Yes
Out-of-court restructurings				
Number of registered cases	234	92	53	825
Number of cases started	157	83	27	430
Number of restructured cases	22	46	10	167
Percentage of restructured debt in total debt	13	40	32	22
In-court restructurings				
Number of registered cases	88	48	52	30
Number of cases started	78	27	34	22
Number of restructured cases	8	19	12	8
Percentage of restructured debt in total debt	4	8	n.a.	7

NOTE: In Thailand, penalties for noncompliance were introduced in August 1999 for creditors who had signed intercreditor agreements

SOURCE: Claessens, Djankov, and Klingebiel (1999).

corporate restructuring has lagged behind financial-sector restructuring. Korea has been the front-runner, having introduced measures to strengthen corporate governance; Indonesia has made the least progress. Even in Korea, however, where there have been reductions in the debt-equity ratios of the largest business conglomerates (*chaebol*), corporate restructuring remains a daunting task. Operational restructuring of ailing corporations has not kept pace with restructuring of their financial obligations in terms of reducing debt-equity ratios (through rescheduling debt and lengthening the maturity of corporate debt). The Asia Recovery Information Centre (ADB-ARIC, 2001b, p. 13) observes that

> ultimately, an improvement in debt servicing capacity requires a return to operational profitability. Progress in operational restructuring of the corporate sector has generally been patchy in all five crisis countries. There are several constraints on operational restructuring of the corporate sectors, including excessive concentration of ownership of businesses, political interference, worker resistance, inadequate insolvency and bankruptcy laws, and ineffective judiciaries.

Notwithstanding efforts to introduce or make more effective bankruptcy laws in all of the Asia-5 countries, the judicial systems in a

14

number of them remain rather weak. The Asia Recovery Information Centre (ADB-ARIC, 2000, p. 22) notes that

> bankruptcy courts, particularly in Indonesia and Thailand, may have difficulty coping with the backlog of cases that is likely to build up. If institutions prove to be ineffective in resolving the debt overhang, this will bode badly for international investment and could again threaten bank capital.... Following restructuring, some debtors have run into difficulties anew. It would seem that the needed operational reforms do not always accompany balance sheet restructuring. Capacity utilization rates are, in general, on the rise, but substantial excess capacity remains in some sectors. Resistance to the painful changes that are required will ultimately have an adverse effect on competitiveness and foreign investor sentiment.

Although crisis countries have made important strides with regard to bank recapitalization and rehabilitation, concerns remain about the future path of policy reforms. There are signs of waning commitments to reform following the global economic slowdown and domestic political concerns, especially in Indonesia.

There can be little room for complacency, particularly because some of the long-term reforms for enhancing the overall efficiency and robustness of the domestic financial system, and also operational corporate restructuring, remain still to be addressed. A partial list of such reforms might include (1) limiting government guarantees and, where these are deemed necessary, ensuring that they are explicit and appropriately priced, (2) diversifying financial systems to reduce dependence on bank intermediation through the development of equity, insurance, and bond markets,[10] (3) enhancing the transparency in the financial system and improving *ex ante* incentives, (4) developing an efficient bankruptcy regime, and (5) strengthening corporate and financial governance structures (such as protecting the rights of minority shareholders).

Although all of these measures are critical, a key difference between the crisis-hit economies (Thailand in particular) and the less affected ones was the lax prudential regulations (either *de facto* or *de jure*) of the private sector in the crisis economies. This is at least partly attributable

---

[10] The need to develop domestic and regional bond markets has been belatedly recognized by the regional economies. The Bank of Thailand's former governor, Chatu Mongol Sonakul (2000), recently noted that "the biggest challenge to us all must be how the crisis could have been avoided in the first place. If [I] can turn back the clock and have a wish, my list may be long. But high in its ranking would be a well functioning Thai baht bond market. . . . [A] bond market provides a basic infrastructure for the development of the financial system and the overall economy. The bond market is an important alternative to bank lending."

to the misunderstanding of the concept of *liberalization* as opposed to *reform*. In the haste to liberalize their economies (and the financial sector, in particular), so as to integrate with the global economy in a market-consistent manner, some of the East Asian economies essentially "threw caution to the wind." A well-functioning market economy does *not* mean no government intervention; financial globalization requires that the government shift its role from active participant (through, for instance, state ownership of banks and other monopolies) to independent, objective mediator, rule-maker, and enforcer. To this end, both a strong and independent bank supervisory function free from political interference and a comprehensive regulatory and supervisory framework are essential. Regulatory measures in this regard include limiting bank exposures to the property sector, strengthening lending guidelines, and ensuring that international banking and accounting standards are met.[11]

Internationalizing the financial system (that is, eliminating discrimination between foreign and domestic financial-services providers) to raise its efficiency may also be an important medium- and longer-term policy measure to enhance the overall efficiency of the banking system. Although the General Agreement on Trade in Services recognizes the right of countries to maintain sovereignty over prudential and related regulations of all financial firms resident in the country (Mattoo, 2000), studies suggest that the introduction of foreign banks into developing countries will create domestic pressure for local banking authorities in these countries to enhance and eventually harmonize regulatory and supervisory procedures and standards to international levels, particularly with regard to risk-management practices (Levine, 1996; Claessens and Glaessner, 1998). Moreover, if the banking system has a more internationally diversified asset base, it might be less prone to instability and financial crisis.[12] There are yet other potential advantages of allowing foreign-bank entry—such as lowering overall financial cost structures—which may make it a desirable policy in and of itself. Some of the regional economies have already taken steps toward internationalizing their financial systems.[13] Care must be taken, however, to ensure that

[11] Mishkin (2000) provides a comprehensive discussion of prudential supervision of financial institutions in emerging economies, with particular reference to crisis prevention.

[12] See IMF (2000, chap. 6) for a balanced and up-to-date discussion of the role of foreign banks in emerging economies. Rajan (2002c) cautions that foreign-bank entry (or privately contracted CCLs) can also be a source of financial contagion.

[13] Montreevat and Rajan (2001) discuss Thailand's recent experience with bank restructuring and foreign-bank entry.

16

foreign competition is introduced gradually in order to avoid disrupting the domestic financial system by enticing domestic banks to opt for increasingly risky investments (that is, "gambling for redemption"). Without such care, an increase in bad loans could offset the efficiency gains associated with greater international competition (Claessens, Demirgüç-Kunt, and Huizinga, 1998; Bird and Rajan, 2001a).

4 Exchange-Rate Policies in Asian Economies

An important component of the Asian financial architecture relates to the choice of exchange-rate regime. Prior to the crisis of 1997–98, Thailand and other regional economies were supposed to have pegged the values of their currencies to a basket comprising the U.S. dollar, the yen, and other currencies, with the weights depending on the linkages with Southeast Asian economies. The reality was, however, that the dollar carried an overwhelming weight, which led to talk of a "dollar standard" or "soft dollar zone" (Tables 5 and 6). The yen had a weight of less than 0.1 in the average Southeast Asian currency basket, despite the fact that Japan was the region's largest export market and largest creditor. This rather rigid pegging to the U.S. dollar is widely perceived as having contributed to the 1997–98 crisis. But what should be drawn from this experience, and have the appropriate policy changes been made?

The consensus view before the crisis was that experience favored the extremes and disfavored the middle ground (Bird, 2002; Rajan, 2002b; and the references therein). The 1990s had been characterized by a series of economic crises that had frequently been associated with attempts by governments to defend pegged exchange rates in conditions of evaporating credibility. According to this consensus, countries should choose either immutably fixed exchange rates, in the form of a close monetary union, in which credibility is assured, or free floating, in which there is no commitment to any particular exchange rate. They should not opt for any regimes lying between these two poles. This consensus has been supported by a series of reports about international monetary reform.[14] There is another point of view, however, suggesting that this is an illegitimate response to the crises of the 1990s and

[14] A report sponsored by the Council on Foreign Relations (Hills, Peterson, and Goldstein, 1999), dealing with reforming the international financial architecture, advises developing countries to "just say no" to pegged exchange rates. Similar advice was proffered by the International Financial Institution Advisory Commission (Meltzer, 2000).

TABLE 5

WEIGHTS OF SELECTED EAST ASIAN CURRENCIES, 1979–1996

	Frankel and Wei (1994)[a]		Kwan (1995)[b]		Kim and Ryou (2001)[c]	
	US$	¥	US$	¥	US$	¥
Indonesian rupiah	0.95	0.16	0.99	0.00	0.97	0.01
Malaysian ringgit	0.78	0.07	0.84	0.04	0.87	0.08
Philippine peso	1.07	−0.01	1.15	−0.24	1.07	0.04
Singapore dollar	0.75	0.13	0.64	0.11	0.68	0.13
Thai baht	0.91	0.05	0.82	0.11	0.82	0.11
Simple average	0.89	0.08	0.88	0.00	0.88	0.07

[a] Based on weekly movements from January 1979 to May 1992.
[b] Based on weekly movements from January 1991 to May 1995.
[c] Based on the period from 1990 to 1996.

TABLE 6

EAST ASIAN EXCHANGE-RATE STATISTICS, 1990–1996

	Domestic Currency per US$1 in 1990		Domestic Currency per US$1 in 1996		Exchange-Rate Variability: Coefficient of Variation, 1990–1996	
	End of Period	Period Average	End of Period	Period Average	End of Period	Period Average
Indonesia	1,901.00	1,842.80	2,383.00	2,342.30	18.94	18.78
Malaysia	2.71	2.70	2.53	2.52	0.00	0.00
Philippines	28.00	24.31	26.29	26.22	0.13	0.13
Thailand	25.52	25.11	25.61	25.49	0.00	0.00

SOURCE: Authors' calculations from IMF, *International Financial Statistics*, various years.

implying that intermediate solutions have not lost all of their appeal. At the same time, moreover, the polar extremes may have their own problems. This alternate view implies that inappropriate conclusions may have been drawn from the evidence. It may be unwise to assume that these "corner solutions" will necessarily avoid future crises. A debate about a new Asian financial architecture needs to be more subtle with respect to the issue of the choice of exchange regime.

The Flexible-Exchange-Rate Option

Reasons to favor flexibility. There are, *a priori*, a number of issues that underlie a preference for greater exchange-rate flexibility. First, the more flexible the exchange-rate regime is, the keener agents will be to undertake appropriate techniques of managing foreign-currency risk in response to the greater levels of exchange-rate risk, while simultaneously reducing the extent of moral hazard that could lead to "excessive" unhedged external borrowing (the so-called "fixed-exchange-rate bubble"). The introduction of these transactions costs and exchange-rate risks may also help moderate the volume of capital inflows, consequently dampening the intensity of boom-and-bust cycles.

Second, banks tend to dominate the financial systems in the region's economies, and the credit-transmission channel plays a significant role. Calvo (1999) has shown that, *ceteris paribus*, the operation of this credit channel (which affects the investment-savings (IS) curve directly and acts as a real shock) could tilt the balance in favor of greater exchange-rate flexibility.

Third, small and open economies are far more susceptible to large external shocks, such as changes in foreign interest rates, terms of trade, regional contagion effects, and the like. Received theory tells us that a greater degree of exchange-rate flexibility is called for in the presence of external or domestic real shocks. By acting as a safety valve, flexible exchange rates provide an adjustment mechanism by which relative prices can be altered in response to such shocks. This is a less costly process than that provided by fixed rates, which rely on gradual reductions in relative costs through deflation and productivity increases vis-à-vis trade partners to restore internal balance—a manner of adjustment that can be both prolonged and extremely costly. Altering the exchange rate is one means of attempting to engender economic adjustment. The need to adjust will depend on the incidence of macroeconomic disequilibria.[15] Related to this, many of the East Asian economies have diversified trade structures (dependent on the United States, Japan, Europe, and intra-Asian trade). Optimum-currency-area (OCA) criteria suggest that such economies are good candidates for maintaining more flexible regimes.

Fourth, it is often suggested that a rigid basket peg may operate as a nominal anchor for monetary policy and may be a way of introducing

[15] Three points should be noted here. One, empirical evidence suggests that pass-through of devaluation is partial; indeed, inflationary predictions were dire in East Asia but did not materialize. Two, devaluation can have real effects in the short term during noncrisis periods. Devaluation during crisis periods appears to be *contractionary* rather than *expansionary* (Hausmann, Panizza, and Stein, 2001; Rajan and Shen, 2001). Three, repeated devaluations will have only price effects but no real effects, because they come to be anticipated by the private sector.

some degree of financial discipline domestically and of breaking inflationary inertia (Edwards, 1993; Bird and Rajan, 2000a). Thus, a study of 136 countries by Ghosh et al. (1995) for the 1960–89 period found that inflation rates generally tend to be greater and more volatile under more flexible regimes, although economic growth is less volatile. An IMF (1997) study of 123 developing countries from 1975 to 1996 arrives at a broadly similar conclusion; that is, the median inflation rate of economies that peg has been consistently lower and less volatile than those that have more flexible arrangements, although the inflation-rate differential between the two sets of economies has decreased throughout the 1990s.[16] Glick, Hutchison, and Moreno (1999), however, have argued that policies of pegging exchange rates in East Asia were of little benefit in terms of acting as a counterinflationary device, this goal having been attained primarily through other factors such as the relative autonomy of the monetary authorities. In the view of these authors, the use of exchange rates as nominal anchors may actually have been a liability, because it prevented the necessary adjustments in response to external shocks. In addition, both theory and lessons of experience with nominal anchors have shown that such pegging loses credibility over time and induces booms followed by inevitable busts and crises (Bird and Rajan, 2000a). Pegging the exchange rate constrains monetary independence.[17] If monetary and fiscal policies have proved effective in the past, governments may be reluctant to constrain their ability to use them in the future by targeting a particular exchange rate. The choice, therefore, depends on the relative merits of alternative macroeconomic policy instruments.

Fifth, it is widely believed that a pegged regime induces increased policy discipline, because fiscal profligacy will lead to a depletion of reserves or to burgeoning debt and an eventual currency collapse. However, the effects of unsound macroeconomic policies become evident immediately under flexible rates through exchange-rate and

---

[16] Although these studies are instructive, they are by no means conclusive, because they do not account for the possibility of endogeneity of the choice exchange-rate regimes. Specifically, we cannot be sure that a fixed exchange rate actually leads to lower inflation or that countries that experience low inflation rates adopt such a regime.

[17] Conversely, if unrestrained monetary policy has been a facet of the country's past, imposing exchange-rate fixity may be an advantage, because it constrains the active use of monetary policy. However, recent empirical evidence casts doubt on the extent to which floating regimes in developing countries provide insulation from foreign-interest-rate shocks (Frankel, Schumkler, and Servén, 2000; Hausmann, Panizza, and Stein, 2001).

price-level movements (the depreciation-inflation spiral). Thus, flexible rates ought to instill greater fiscal restraint and discipline, because the costs of macroeconomic policy transgressions have to be paid up front. In other words, the key distinction between fixed and floating rates is in the intertemporal distribution of costs and benefits (Tornell and Velasco, 2000). Gavin and Perotti (1997) provide some empirical validity to this argument.

Reasons for a "fear of floating." Despite the preceding arguments favoring a flexible-exchange-rate regime, countries with flexible regimes appear to have experienced "excessive" volatility over the last few decades.[18] It is admittedly difficult to define exactly what is meant by the term "excessive." However, a reading of the literature on available empirical studies of exchange rates reveals that evidence of excessive exchange-rate variability comes in a number of forms (Williamson, 1999b; Bird and Rajan, 2001b, 2001c). For instance, a number of surveys of foreign-exchange-market participants clearly indicate that short-term, high-frequency exchange-rate movements are caused by "speculative" or "trend-following" elements, rather than by underlying macroeconomic fundamentals. The problem of destabilizing speculation and consequent excessive exchange-rate volatility appears to be exacerbated in developing countries, making a flexible regime especially unviable or unsuitable for them (Grenville and Gruen, 1999). This is particularly so because thin markets, which exist in Southeast Asia and other developing countries (Table 7), imply that a few transactions can lead to extreme exchange-rate fluctuations.

Even if it were accepted that flexible exchange rates often appear to exhibit greater volatility in high-frequency data than would be warranted by the underlying fundamentals, why might such excessive volatility be of concern? Recent studies have provided evidence of a negative impact of exchange-rate volatility and uncertainty on investment (Huizinga, 1994; Corbo and Cox, 1997).[19] To the extent that investment has a significant positive impact on economic growth, declining investment

---

[18] Of course, no country has maintained a completely free (or pure) float, because the authorities have intervened intermittently to smooth market fluctuations. In other words, "dirty floats"—that is, foreign-exchange-market interventions without commitment to defend any specific parity—have been the norm. The U.S. dollar probably comes closest to being a free float.

[19] Corbo and Cox (1997) and others also find that macroeconomic uncertainty in general has a deleterious impact on investment. See, also, Servén's (1997) broad survey of the literature.

21

TABLE 7

FOREIGN-EXCHANGE-MARKET ACTIVITY IN SELECTED EAST ASIAN
AND INDUSTRIAL ECONOMIES
(*US$ billions*)

	GDP (1997)	Average Daily Turnover of Foreign-Exchange Activity (as of April 1998)	Ratio of Average Daily Turnover to GDP (%)
Indonesia	214.6	1.5	0.7
Malaysia	97.9	1.1	1.1
Thailand	153.9	3.0	2.0
Germany	2,102.6	94.3	4.5
Japan	4,192.3	148.6	3.5
Switzerland	254.9	81.7	15.5
United Kingdom	1,288.4	637.6	49.5
United States	8,111.0	350.9	4.3

SOURCE: Min and McDonald (1999).

will have an enduring adverse effect on the quantity of real resources. Even in the absence of a negative effect on the level of investment, exchange-rate variability may adversely affect the composition of investment, because decisions might be based on disequilibrium prices.

It has often been argued that firms and other agents involved in international transactions can undertake hedging operations to shield themselves against exchange-rate movements. However, apart from the costs involved with such operations, perfect hedges may be very difficult to create technically, given acute revenue-cost uncertainties (Adler, 1996; Friberg, 1997). Indeed, even if they could be created, they would entail non-negligible transaction costs, thus diverting scarce resources from "real" economic activity. This is especially true in the case of developing countries, where rudimentary capital markets have necessitated using cross-hedging techniques (rather than direct hedging), which invariably are far costlier. A 1992 survey of nonfinancial Fortune 500 corporations finds that although 85 percent of the respondents hedged, only 22 per cent hedged *fully*. Not surprisingly, most of the respondents that did not hedge were smaller firms averaging US$2 billion in capital (Felix, 1996; Felix and Sau, 1996). It is important to remember that such small and medium-sized enterprises dominate the economic landscape in developing countries.

In a cross-sectional study of bilateral trade, Frankel and Wei (1994) find that bilateral-exchange-rate variability seems to have had a statistically and economically significant negative effect on trade between 1960 and 1985, although the impact—both statistical and economic—has been negligible between 1985 and 1990.[20] Wei (1999) provides new empirical evidence suggesting that exchange-rate volatility has damaged trade between pairs of countries to a much larger extent than is suggested by previous studies. More generally, McKenzie (1999, p. 100), in a comprehensive survey of the literature on the impact of exchange-rate volatility on trade flows, concludes that the recent empirical studies have had "greater success in deriving a statistically significant relationship between volatility and trade." Calvo and Reinhart (2000) review a more limited set of such studies and draw a similar conclusion. Another recent set of empirics by Rose, based on gravity models using both cross-sectional and time-series data, suggests that institutionally fixed exchange regimes in general, but a common currency in particular, stimulate trade, which in turn boosts income (Frankel and Rose, 2000; Rose, 2000; Glick and Rose, 2001). As is common knowledge, proponents of the European economic and monetary union (EMU) used such an argument extensively. Flexible exchange rates may also be associated with currency misalignments, with accompanying costs in terms of resource misallocation, and with detrimental effects on economic growth.

Notwithstanding the recent weakness of the Australian dollar,[21] Australia's successful experience with a floating arrangement, particularly in terms of withstanding the East Asian crisis, has often been cited as evidence of the "superiority" of such a regime and has sometimes been held up as a model for Southeast Asian countries. Such advocacy, however, does not pay due consideration to the fact that there are important structural differences between industrial countries such as Australia, and developing countries (Krugman, 1999). For instance, countries such as Australia and the United States have well-developed and diversified financial systems that are able to minimize real-sector disruptions caused by transitory exchange-rate variations (abstracting from the resource-allocation costs of the misalignments noted above). Most important, industrial countries are able to borrow overseas in their domestic currencies. Many developing countries are unable to do so, leading to the accumulation of foreign-currency debt

[20] On balance, these earlier time-series studies seem to have found an insignificant effect of exchange-rate uncertainty on trade; see Willett's (1986) synopsis of the literature.

[21] The Australian dollar lost half of its U.S. dollar value between the end of 1996 and early 2001. *The Economist* (April 29, 2000, p. 84) discusses the reasons behind this fall in value.

23

liabilities that are primarily dollar denominated and unhedged (that is, "liability dollarization").[22] In such countries, sharp depreciations in their currencies alter the domestic-currency value of their external debt and, therefore, the net worth of their economies, causing adverse real-sector effects (so-called "balance-sheet" effects). This may explain the "fear of floating" exhibited by many developing countries (Calvo and Reinhart, 2000, 2001; Hausmann, Panizza, and Stein, 2001). This fear has, in turn, led to growing enthusiasm for the other corner solution, an irrevocably fixed regime. Such a hard peg, it is argued, signals a greater commitment to rule out arbitrary exchange-rate adjustments (that is, "escape clauses" cannot be invoked), as well as the authorities' willingness to subordinate domestic-policy objectives such as output and employment growth to the maintenance of the pegged exchange rate. Hard pegs can assume a number of forms; would these work in Asia?

Currency Boards and Dollarization

The durability of the Hong Kong and Argentine currency boards in the face of acute speculative pressures in the 1990s appears to have convinced some observers of the virtues of currency boards for a number of developing countries, including those in Southeast Asia. In fact, the *Asian Monetary Monitor* (July-August 1994, pp. 1–10) had suggested such a regime for the regional countries precrisis, and Indonesia toyed with the idea during the early part of 1998.[23] Others argue that developing countries should form a monetary union with the United States, or more specifically, that they ought to abandon their respective national currencies in favor of the U.S. dollar—that is, they should dollarize (Hausmann, 1999).[24]

---

[22] This has come to be referred to as the "original sin" hypothesis, a term attributed to Hausmann (1999) and Hausmann, Panizza, and Stein (2001). It is unclear why many developing countries are unable to borrow long-term in their own currencies. McLean and Shreshta (2001) explore this issue using a case-study approach involving Australia, New Zealand, and South Africa, all small and open economies that borrow internationally in domestic currencies. They conclude that countries in which domestic long-term government debt is widely held by residents are more likely to convince nonresidents to hold debt denominated in local currencies. They further suggest that the development of the Eurobond markets for debt denominated in Australian dollars, New Zealand dollars, and the South African rand were instrumental in fortifying international access to debt denominated in the domestic currencies of those countries.

[23] See Culp, Hanke, and Miller (1999) in defense of, and Spiegel (1998) for the case against, a currency board in Indonesia.

[24] The relative merits of dollarization over a currency board are not discussed here (see, instead, Frankel, 1999; Berg and Borensztein, 2000; and Frankel, Schumkler, and

It is generally recognized that such hard pegs require the satisfaction of a number of preconditions (Frankel, 1999), including the presence of a strong and durable domestic financial system that can withstand possible interest-rate hikes on a sustained basis during periods when the domestic currency is under selling pressure. Failing this, currency-crisis vulnerability might merely become financial-sector vulnerability (this point is formalized by Chang and Velasco, 1998). To the extent that the banking systems in the regional countries have been decimated by the crisis and the process of financial-sector restructuring (though having progressed substantially) is far from complete, the currency-board alternative seems to be infeasible for the near to medium term. This is particularly so because the elimination of the lender-of-last-resort (LOLR) function of a central bank by the introduction of a currency board implies the need for a strong, well-capitalized, and well-supervised domestic financial system.[25]

There is also the question of whether the regional countries have a sufficient degree of labor-market and internal flexibility (as Hong Kong has, for instance) to make such a super fix viable. Without such flexibility, a currency-board arrangement makes adjustments to large economic shocks extremely costly. In such circumstances, forsaking the exchange rate as a policy tool is certainly not an appealing option.[26] A great deal has been made of Hong Kong's ability to maintain its U.S. dollar-based

---

Servén, 2000). Suffice it to note that the chief advantage of dollarization is a reduction in the currency-risk premium, and possibly even the country-risk premium, thereby offering lower domestic interest rates, as well as the elimination of concerns about the sustainability of the domestic currency peg (that is, no escape clause). The major disadvantages of moving from a currency-board arrangement to dollarization are the loss of seigniorage, constraints on liquidity management, and the transition costs.

[25] The loss of a domestic LOLR function may be partly compensated for by holding excess reserves (over and above the domestic monetary base), as in the case of Hong Kong, or by obtaining access to foreign credit lines, as in the case of Argentina. A referee points out that the LOLR function need not necessarily be assigned to the central bank. What matters in the end is the ability to tax current and future generations and to provide current liquidity in exchange. Such a role could lie with an independent fiscal authority.

[26] The point is sometimes made that these preconditions are not necessary for the implementation of a currency board or dollarization (which overlap considerably). No doubt either arrangement can be implemented prior to reforms, but what are the implications of doing so? It is useful to remember that the failure to pay sufficient attention to the preconditions for successful financial liberalization has been among the main reasons for financial crises in developing countries. Eichengreen (2002) provides a detailed review of the dollarization literature and discusses at some length the preconditions needed for implementation.

currency-board arrangement in the midst of acute bearish pressure in 1997–98. Much less recognized is the fact that Singapore, which pursued a monitoring-band arrangement of the Williamson (1999b) type precrisis and continues to do so postcrisis,[27] weathered the East Asian crisis comparatively well, despite having extremely strong direct trade and financial links with most of the crisis-hit regional economies (Rajan, Sen, and Siregar, 2002).[28]

In addition, it is revealing that both Argentina and Hong Kong have themselves recently advocated that their regions explore alternative hard-peg arrangements—dollarization, in the case of Latin America, and East Asian monetary cooperation, or at least coordination, in the case of Hong Kong. Cynics of currency-board arrangements have interpreted this interest as a search by the two economies for viable exit strategies from their respective currency-board arrangements. The Argentine case is especially revealing. Although Argentina's hard peg to the U.S. dollar was important in helping the country realize financial and monetary stability, the recent large shocks in emerging-market economies (Mexico in 1994–95, East Asia in 1997–98, and Brazil in 1999) required exchange-rate adjustments that, until January 2002, were not forthcoming. This, in turn, necessitated extremely painful internal adjustments in Argentina that eventually rendered the country's currency-board arrangement a politically unacceptable liability (Rajan, 2002a).

Although a policy of formal dollarization may have some merit in Latin America (Bird, 2001a), the comparatively low levels of informal dollarization in Southeast Asia and the economically significant role played by Japan and the yen in both Southeast Asia and the larger East

---

[27] The Monetary Authority of Singapore (www.mas.gov.sg) describes the management of its exchange-rate policy as follows:

MAS manages the Singapore dollar against a basket of currencies of Singapore's main trading partners and competitors. The basket is composed of the currencies of those countries that are the main sources of imported inflation and competition in export markets. . . . The trade-weighted Singapore dollar is allowed to float within an undisclosed target band. The level and width of the band are reviewed periodically to ensure that they are consistent with economic fundamentals and market conditions. The MAS intervenes in the foreign exchange market from time to time to ensure that movements of the [Singapore dollar] exchange rate are orderly and consistent with the exchange rate policy.

[28] Although Hong Kong's overall GDP declined by 5 percent in 1998, Singapore's growth stagnated at 0.4 percent. The primary reason for this difference is that in Singapore, the nominal-exchange-rate flexibility was able to cushion some of the negative shock, whereas in Hong Kong, adjustments in the real exchange rate had to be fully realized through domestic deflation (Rajan and Siregar, 2000).

Asia imply that dollarization (let alone euroization or yenization) may not be a viable option for this region. An important lesson from the East Asian crisis of 1997–98 is that if the regional economies had given greater weight to the yen when managing their currencies, there would have been lower degrees of regional real-exchange-rate overvaluations following the nearly 50 percent nominal appreciation of the U.S. dollar relative to the yen between June 1995 and April 1997 (which in turn led to an appreciation of the regional currencies relative to the yen).[29] In the case of Thailand, which was the "crisis trigger country," for instance, various studies have suggested that the Thai baht's precrisis real effective exchange rate was misaligned ("overvalued") by 11 to 30 percent relative to some measure of the "equilibrium" real exchange rate (Montiel, 1999; Rajan, Sen, and Siregar, 2000; Rajan, 2001a). Institutionalization of the dollar pegs (through a currency board or dollarization) would not have helped domestic economic performance, to the extent that the problem reflected, at least partly, a loss of competitiveness. Consistent with this conclusion, a recent study of exports performance of about 100 developing countries trading with the United States, Japan, and Europe from 1983 to 1992 concludes that the more flexible the exchange-rate regime, the better the export performance (Nilsson and Nilsson, 2000). However, data based on the official IMF classification of exchange-rate arrangements, that is, *de jure*, rather than *de facto*, exchange-rate regimes, suggest that countries pegging to a composite group of currencies have not underperformed countries with independently floating regimes.

Monetary Union

Having experienced the turbulence of the regional crisis and with the introduction of a single European currency as a backdrop, leaders of the Association of Southeast Asian Nations (ASEAN) have agreed to study the feasibility of a common ASEAN currency system.[30] There has been much popular discussion in the region about the possibility of forming an Asian monetary union. From an economic standpoint, Eichengreen and Bayoumi (1999a, 1999b) have concluded that East Asia may be as close to, or as far away from, being an OCA as Western

---

[29] McKinnon (2001) refers to the yen-U.S. dollar exchange rate as the "loose cannon" in precrisis East Asia.

[30] This was announced as part of the sixth ASEAN summit meeting in Hanoi in 1998 and included in the "Hanoi Plan of Action" (*Business Times* [Singapore], December 15, 1998).

Europe is.[31] This conclusion is based on an OCA index that takes into account the costs associated with asymmetric region-wide shocks as well as the benefits from stabilizing exchange rates with trading partners.[32] More informally, but in a similar vein, the IMF's managing director, Horst Köhler (2001, p. 4), has noted that "trading patterns and geography do make it reasonable to think of the creation of an internal market in Asia as a possible, future stage in regional cooperation. And why should this not be a basis for greater monetary integration?"

There are, however, at least two important differences between East Asia and Europe. First, in the absence of sufficiently frictionless intraregional labor mobility, any form of regional monetary union requires that there be compensating fiscal transfers from the richer to the poorer states. In the case of Europe, the extent of such transfers is quite significant in per capita terms for the poorer states but fairly low in absolute terms, because the richer states in Europe are much larger than the poorer ones (Eichengreen and Bayoumi, 1999a, 1999b). This is in contrast to developing East Asia, where the poorer regional members also happen to be the largest (China and Indonesia, as opposed to Singapore).

Second, the European experience has emphasized the need for strong political will and consensus toward such a policy goal. Indeed, some observers, such as Goodhart (1995), dispute the relevance of economic criteria altogether, claiming that political considerations dominate the formation of currency areas. Although such a political consensus may gradually emerge in Southeast Asia and the larger East Asian region, it is still some way off. "Vision statements" by regional leaders in favor of currency union have become more common since the crisis, but they have hitherto not been supported by any serious discussion about what kind of institutional structures or formal mechanisms and decisionmaking bodies are needed for such regional economic integration (for example, an independent region-wide central bank, a system of interregional fiscal transfers, and measures to ensure macroeconomic convergence). Eichengreen and Bayoumi (1999b, p. 11) have noted that "there is little sign, comparable to the evidence which has existed in Europe for nearly 50 years, of a willingness to subordinate

---

[31] Similarly, Rockoff (2000) has emphasized that the United States can be said to have been an OCA only during the 1930s. See Kenen (2000) for a recent discussion of OCA theory.

[32] It is also possible that OCA criteria may be at least partly endogenous, suggesting that some unions may be more justifiable *ex post* than *ex ante* (Frankel and Rose, 1998).

national prerogatives to some larger regional entity. There is no wider web of interlocking arrangements, as in the EU, which would be put at risk by a failure to follow through on promises of monetary and financial cooperation."[33] Thus, the general conclusion offered by Kenen (2000) that the problems of governance and accountability may prove inseparable for most non-European groups of countries appears especially pertinent to East Asia.

The Revealed Preferences of East Asian Central Banks

What exchange-rate policies have been pursued in East Asia in the postcrisis period? Is there any evidence of the so-called "fear of floating." The Malaysian case is the most straightforward, with the government fixing the Malaysian ringitt at RM 3.80 per US $1 on September 1, 1998 (Athukorala, 2001; Kaplan and Rodrik, 2001). More interesting and somewhat more complicated are the exchange-rate choices of the other three regional economies. It is commonly believed that Indonesia, the Philippines, and Thailand have maintained a float following their respective currency devaluations. In actuality, however, after a short flirtation with floating following the initial breakdown of currency pegs in mid-1997, the regional monetary authorities appear to have reverted to heavy management of their currencies to ensure some degree of stability with respect to the U.S. dollar. To be sure, there has been a generalized move toward greater exchange-rate flexibility during the postcrisis period (see Figure 1 and Hernandez and Montiel, 2001). However, although the Malaysian capital controls have allowed for simultaneously maintaining both monetary autonomy and a fixed-rate regime, the other East Asian economies have depended on a combination of activist interest-rate policy and foreign-exchange-market intervention to ensure relative-exchange-rate stability. They have consequently experienced sharp gyrations in monetary variables and international reserves (Calvo and Reinhart, 2000, 2001; Hernandez and Montiel, 2001; McKinnon, 2001). Consistent with this finding, it is useful to note the following statement by Thailand's finance minister, Pridiyathorn Devakula:

---

[33] In addition, substantial asymmetries in the sizes, levels, and stages of economic development of the countries in East Asia and the *de facto* policy of strict nonintervention in one another's economic and, particularly, political affairs makes it extremely difficult to envisage the successful introduction of EMU-like "tie-in" clauses to create punishment mechanisms to ensure conformity of economic policies.

FIGURE 1

BILATERAL EXCHANGE RATES OF THE ASIA-5 CURRENCIES RELATIVE TO THE U.S. DOLLAR, 1996–2001

(June 1997 = 100)

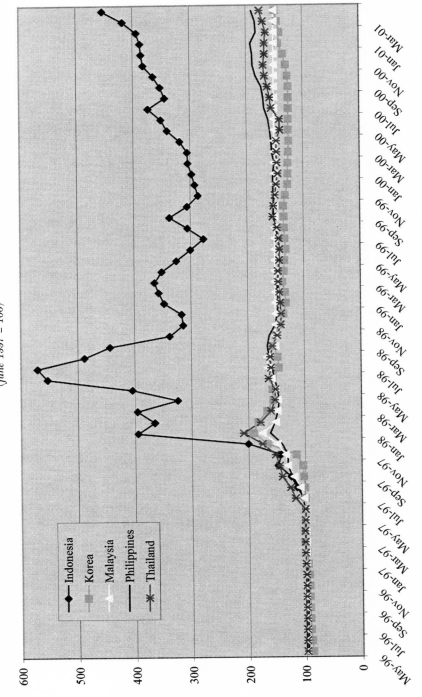

(W)e are using the stabilised exchange rate as one of the guiding principles. Why do we have to use this? It's simple—there are two extremes: fixed exchange rate and clean float. . . . (M)y attitude to fixed exchange rates— don't do it. If you do, you invite trouble and finally lose all your reserves. The other is clean float. If we were strong like the U.S., Japan, Germany we would go clean float. Because a clean float rate can swing to extremes, it can savage our current account. When the economy is weakening and confidence of private businessmen is not that high, we must make sure our currency does not swing to the extreme where it creates panic. That's why we have to choose the middle road (*Far Eastern Economic Review*, July 26, 2001, pp. 50–51).

More evidence of this disinclination to allow the exchange rate to float freely is seen in the fact that the regional economies began reaccumulating international-reserve holdings following the sharp declines in 1997. East Asian economies have rapidly built up international reserves in the postcrisis period—commonly termed "floating with a life-jacket" (see Figure 2; Hernandez and Montiel, 2001; and Park, 2001). The replenishment and accumulation of international reserves, as well as the lengthening of the average maturity profile of the regional economies' external indebtedness (Table 8), has significantly reduced the region's vulnerability to the destabilizing effects of volatile and easily reversible capital flows.[34] Nonetheless, recent weaknesses in the regional currencies and the desire by the central banks to offset at least part of the currency declines against the U.S. dollar have led to a slight drain in reserves in some of the regional economies since late 2000 (Figure 2 and ADB-ARIC, 2001).

Summing up, Hernandez and Montiel (2001, p. 16), who analyze the evidence regarding the postcrisis exchange-rate policies pursued in the Asia-5 economies, conclude that

contrary to the views of some observers, . . . there has indeed been a change in *de facto* exchange rate regimes in all five of these countries between the pre- and post-crisis periods. While none of them have adopted

[34] The extent of short-term indebtedness has been found to be a key indicator of (il)liquidity and a robust predictor of financial crises (Bussière and Mulder, 1999; Rodrik and Velasco, 1999; World Bank, 1999; Dadush, Dasgupta, and Ratha, 2000). According to Dadush, Dasgupta, and Ratha, on the basis of data for thirty-three developing economies, the elasticity of short-term debt with GDP growth is 0.9 when there is a positive shock to output and −1.8 when there is a negative shock. This extreme reversibility of short-term debt in the event of negative shock exposes borrowers to liquidity runs and systemic crises. In a somewhat contrarian view, Jeanne (2000) argues that it is not clear that short-term-debt contracts ought to be discouraged, because they may play a socially advantageous function in reducing agency problems.

FIGURE 2

INDEX OF GROSS INTERNATIONAL RESERVES, LESS GOLD, IN THE ASIA-5 ECONOMIES, 1997–2001

(June 1997 = 100)

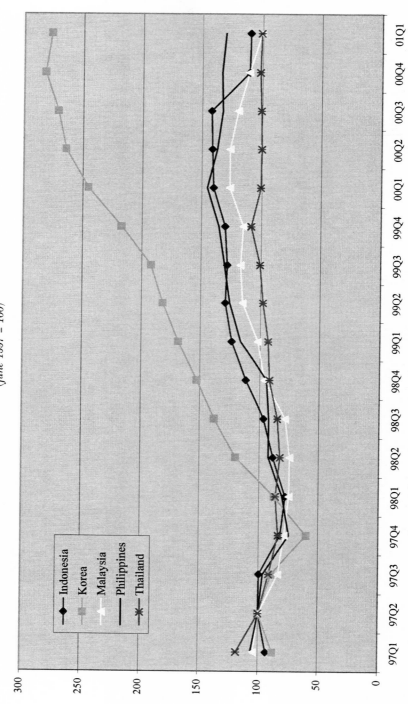

TABLE 8

EXTERNAL DEBT OF THE EAST ASIAN ECONOMIES, 1995–1999

(Percent of GDP)

	1995	1996	1997	1998	1999	2000
Indonesia[a]	56.3	53.4	63.9	149.4	95.5	93.8
Korea	26.0	31.6	33.4	46.9	33.4	26.5
Malaysia	37.6	38.4	43.8	58.8	53.4	49.3
Philippines	54.9	55.0	61.6	81.7	75.7	78.9
Thailand	49.1	49.8	62.0	76.9	61.4	51.7
Of Which, Short-Term Debt						
Indonesia[a]	8.7	7.5	27.5	76.4	5.9	5.7
Korea	14.6	17.9	23.1	9.7	9.3	7.7
Malaysia	7.2	9.9	11.1	11.7	7.6	6.4
Philippines	8.3	12.0	14.0	15.6	11.3	7.5
Thailand	24.5	20.7	13.3	21.0	11.4	6.8

[a] Data for Indonesia exclude trade credits.
SOURCE: IMF (2000).

"soft pegs" with unfettered capital movements, neither have they moved to the extreme corner solutions of "hard" pegs or clean floats. In other words, all of them have continued to manage their exchange rates in an active manner, and have thus occupied the supposed "hollow middle" of exchange rate policy.

The Choice of Exchange-Rate Regime Reconsidered

But what exchange-rate regime should form part of an evolving Asian financial architecture? The preceding discussion leads to the unsatisfying conclusion that when it comes to selecting the appropriate exchange-rate regime, all that can really be said is that there is a broad spectrum of choice (Frankel, 1999; Mussa et al., 2000; and Bird, 2002, reach broadly similar conclusions). Frankel (1999) has provided us with two timely reminders: (1) the "impossible trinity or trilogy" does not on its own imply that in an increasingly globalized world economy, an intermediate regime is unviable; (2) few developing countries appear to meet the OCA criteria to make either corner solution an ideal choice, and "one size does not fit all" (see also Kenen, 2000; Willett, 2001b; and Bird, 2002).

Choosing the exchange-rate regime should represent a consistent part of a coherent macroeconomic strategy. If not viewed in this way, any regime is likely to fail because inconsistencies will arise. No exchange-rate regime will deliver stability if domestic macroeconomic policy is unsound, yielding large fiscal deficits and rapid monetary growth and inflation. Pegged exchange rates will become overvalued and reserves will fall, and flexible exchange rates will depreciate and possibly trigger crises. Exchange-rate policy in emerging economies may need to have a more limited objective. Rather than focusing on disciplining domestic macroeconomic policy and labor markets, the exchange-rate regime should perhaps be designed in the first instance to minimize exposure to the third-currency phenomenon, in which the problem for emerging economies arises from fluctuations in the values of the currencies of their major trading partners against each other.

In the absence of strong capital controls, currency intervention ought not to be framed as a specific target for the exchange rate. Such targets inevitably tempt speculators by offering them the infamous one-way option. Thus, exchange-rate and monetary-policy strategies must involve an element of flexibility, rather than a single-minded defense of a particular rate. This might best be achieved by a Singapore-type variant on sliding parities and wider bands around an appropriately weighted currency basket—a band-basket-crawl (BBC)[35]—or by a more flexible exchange rate combined with an inflation target.[36] Neither of these strategies supports the benign neglect of the exchange rate.

5 Regional Liquidity Arrangements

Financial Crisis and the Importance of Liquidity

Currency-crisis models suggest the circumstances under which exchange rates are likely to come under speculative attack (Rajan, 2001). If the authorities wish to prevent the full impact of the selling of a currency on its value, they have to buy it. In order to do so, they need foreign exchange, and this may come from decumulating international reserves or from foreign borrowing. The problem is that reserve decumulation

[35] The crawl is meant to compensate for inflation differentials. Williamson (1999b) discusses the BBC policy in some detail, and Williamson (1999a) and Rajan (2002b) explore this option for East Asia.

[36] Many central banks that purport to operate an inflation target actually pursue a flexible version of it. This is clear from the fact that in most cases, the official monetary-policy stance is captured by a Monetary Conditions Index, which is a weighted average of the interest rate and the exchange rate. Eichengreen (2001a) discusses in some depth definitions and issues surrounding a monetary-policy strategy organized around an inflation target.

has a finite limit, and private capital, by definition, will be exiting. It is in these circumstances that developing and emerging economies may be forced to turn to the IMF.

An important dimension of any crisis is likely to be illiquidity. Illiquidity can create crises even where the economic fundamentals are sound, or it can make a bad situation worse when the fundamentals are weak. Once it becomes a problem, moreover, illiquidity further undermines the confidence of international capital markets. Capital outflows increase, thereby reducing liquidity still further. Currency-crisis models have shown that once countries fall below some liquidity threshold, matters can deteriorate rapidly (Chang and Velasco, 1998). Although there continues to be debate about the extent to which fundamentals accounted for the East Asian crisis, there is little doubt that illiquidity was a part of the problem. Prior to the crisis, capital inflows exceeded deficits in the current-account balance of payments, and this allowed international reserves to be accumulated. As capital markets lost confidence, however, capital inflows suddenly became capital outflows, and the reserves were run down as a way of financing current-account deficits. Confidence declined still further as reserves were depleted; a trickle became a flood; and countries in the region were forced to turn to the IMF for financial assistance.

Although large in relation to the IMF's normal lending, the loans from the IMF did not come close to compensating fully for the outflows of private capital. This implied the need to switch from a policy of financing current-account deficits to a policy of correcting them. The speed and intensity of economic adjustment in East Asia in 1998 was largely dictated by the shortage of liquidity. Indeed, it was the extreme shortage of liquidity that called for rapid adjustment.[37]

Some indication of the degree of adjustment may be gleaned from examining what happened to output and real exchange rates following the financial crisis (Figures 3 and 4). Traditional balance-of-payments theory distinguishes between expenditure-switching and expenditure-changing policies, and it is tempting to portray exchange-rate devaluation (the classic expenditure-switching device) as an alternative to

---

[37] Thus, Eichengreen and Rose (2001) argue that the East Asian process of V-shaped adjustment has not been very different from the stylized patterns of previous currency-crisis episodes in developing countries. However, the degree of the initial contraction and following recovery has been far greater in East Asia and can be attributed to the severe liquidity crisis that was triggered by investors' panic (Park, 2001a; Rajan and Siregar, 2002).

FIGURE 3

THE QUARTERLY GDP GROWTH RATES IN THE ASIA-5 ECONOMIES, 1996–2001

(*Percent year-on-year*)

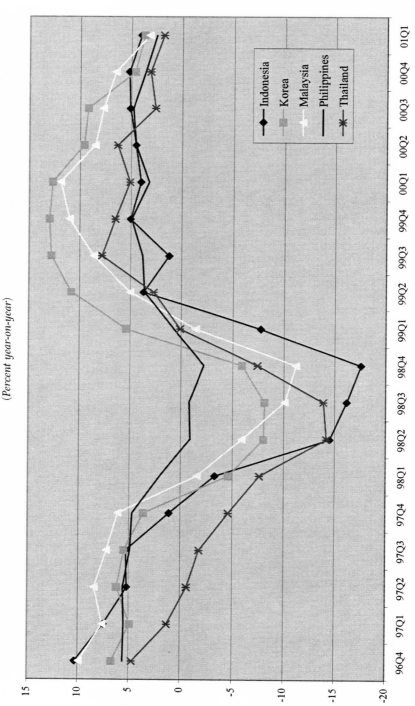

FIGURE 4

REAL EFFECTIVE EXCHANGE RATES FOR THE ASIA-5 CURRENCIES, 1994–2001

(*January 1994 = 100*)

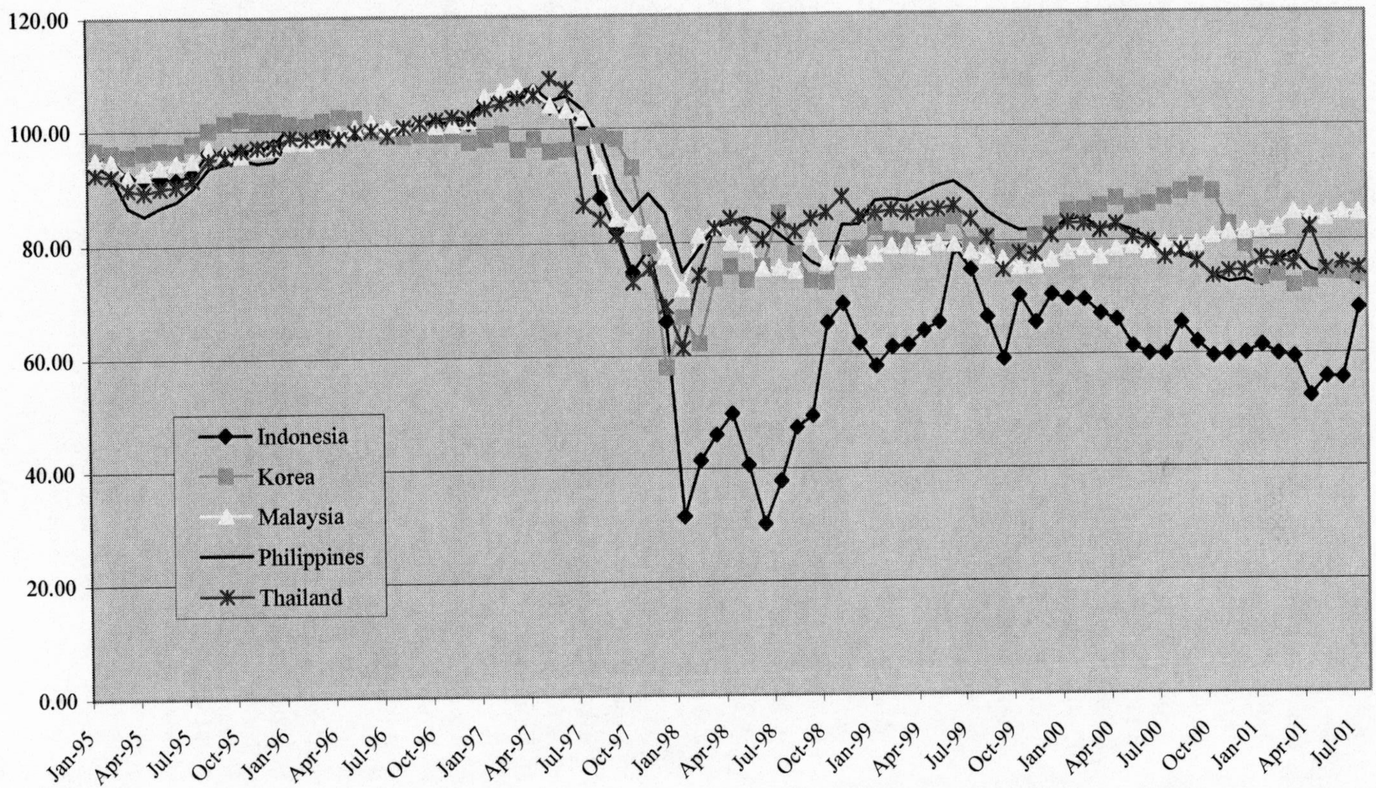

contractionary expenditure policies. If this were the case, it might be supposed that the East Asian economies would have experienced a sharp fall in either the values of their currencies or output but not both. As it happened, however, the balance-sheet effects of devaluation for the domestic financial and corporate sectors seem to have created temporary but sharp recessionary repercussions, because there was a rapid rise in the domestic currency cost of servicing obligations denominated in foreign currencies and a domestic liquidity crunch (Krugman, 1999; Bird and Rajan, 2000c; Boorman et al., 2000; Rajan and Shen, 2001). To the extent that the recessionary effects of devaluation were underestimated at the time, contractionary-aggregate-demand management policies would have resulted in recession overkill. Judged against potential output (real GDP) for each economy, the IMF (1999) has estimated that the cumulative four-year output losses from the 1997–98 crisis were much larger than those following the Tequila crisis in Latin America in 1994, ranging from a low of 27 percent of total "potential" output in Korea to a high of 82 percent in Indonesia.[38] The question then becomes, could these output losses have been reduced? This brings us back to the trade-off between the severity of adjustment in the short run and the availability of international liquidity.

International Liquidity, Crisis Prevention, and the IMF

As already noted, illiquidity, lack of confidence, and self-fulfilling expectations create a highly combustible cocktail. But, by the same token, where liquidity is *perceived* to be adequate, confidence might be maintained and the self-fulfillment of expectations may mean that liquidity *is* adequate. It has long been recognized that inadequate liquidity can threaten the stability of international financial regimes. Thus, during the 1960s, the prime concern about the Bretton Woods international financial system was the widely perceived shortage of international liquidity. A sequence of reforms designed to increase

---

[38] The cumulative loss is calculated as the sum of the output gap over a four-year period, starting with the crisis year. The output gap is defined as the percent difference between the actual and the hypothetical (or potential) level of real GDP for each country. Graphically, the cumulative output loss would thus be represented by the area between the potential and actual output paths, starting from the crisis year and expressed as a percentage of potential real GDP. It follows that accumulated losses will be positive, and possibly large, even in cases where output is back to potential at the end of the four-year period. In the counterfactual scenario, it is assumed that potential GDP grows at 4 percent per annum and that actual and potential output coincided within the two-year period preceding the crisis.

international liquidity—culminating in the introduction of the IMF's own international reserve asset, the Special Drawing Right (SDR)—was aimed at shoring up the Bretton Woods system by reducing its vulnerability to crisis. Prior to the establishment of the SDR, the IMF attempted to provide quick-disbursing low-conditionality finance through lower credit tranche drawings and through its Compensatory Financing Facility (CFF), which was designed to help countries deal with problems caused by exogenous shortfalls in export earnings. Although the CFF was designed with developing countries in mind, the industrial countries developed a system of bilateral swap arrangements within which countries encountering a speculative crisis threatening the durability of their exchange-rate peg could swap domestic currency for foreign currency from other central banks—a transaction that would be reversed after the speculative attack had been repelled and the crisis had passed. Ultimately, industrial countries no longer needed to turn to the IMF for assistance, because they managed to develop sources of liquidity that they deemed preferable.

An obvious method of enhancing a country's liquidity position is through the accumulation of international reserves. As Fischer (2001a, pp. 1–3) notes,

> reserves matter because they are a key determinant of a country's ability to avoid economic and financial crisis. This is true of all countries, but especially of emerging markets open to volatile international capital flows. . . . The availability of capital flows to offset current account shocks should, on the face of it, reduce the amount of reserves a country needs. But access to private capital is often uncertain, and inflows are subject to rapid reversals, as we have seen all too often in recent years. We have also seen in the recent crises that countries that had big reserves by and large did better in withstanding contagion than those with smaller reserves.

An important limitation of such a reserve-hoarding policy is that it involves high fiscal costs, because the country effectively swaps high-yielding domestic assets for lower-yielding foreign assets.[39] In addition,

---

[39] There is the additional question of what the appropriate size of reserve holdings should be. Against what yardstick should reserve adequacy be measured? The generally accepted rule of thumb that a country needs to hold reserves equivalent to short-term debt cover (that is, debt that actually falls due during the year) is true only in the case in which a country is running a current-account deficit and there are no other liabilities that are easily reversible (Fischer, 2001a). The optimal level of reserves depends on a number of factors, such as degree of export diversification, size and variability of the current-account imbalance, and type of exchange-rate regime used (Bussière and Mulder, 1999).

because the size of international reserve holdings has been found to be a theoretically and statistically significant determinant of creditworthiness (Haque, 1996; Bussière and Mulder, 1999; Disyatat, 2001), depleting these holdings as a way of cushioning the effect of capital outflows on the exchange rate may make matters worse by inducing further capital outflows. If capital outflows reflect a perception within private capital markets that a country is illiquid, reducing international reserves and thereby curbing liquidity further is hardly likely to be an effective strategy. In other words, the reversibility that makes reserve depletion credible in the context of current-account deficits is often absent in the context of capital outflows.

From a government's perspective, one advantage associated with international reserves is that they may be used quickly and without conditions. This may also appear to be true of financing from private-capital markets. But although private-capital inflows may, again, logically be used to finance temporary deficits in the current-account balance of payments, the logic breaks down when the crisis is connected to the capital account.[40] In this case, it is capital outflows that are part of the problem. Countries will be losing creditworthiness and, consequently, their access to private-capital markets. Liquidity-based policies will, instead, have to be directed toward arresting the outflow of capital. In the midst of the crisis, there is no guarantee that conventional wisdom relating to the capital account will apply. Thus, raising the rate of interest may transmit a negative signal about the state of the economy and its future prospects and may lead to further capital outflows.[41] A fall in the value of the currency may enhance expectations of a further fall, with a similar outcome.

A related issue pertains to the appropriate currency composition of reserves in terms of currency composition (Eichengreen and Mathieson, 2000). Steps have been taken to improve the IMF's analytical framework for management of international reserves, as well as to assess a country's external financial vulnerability in general (IMF, 2001a, chap. 3).

[40] In recognition of the urgent need to study and understand further the workings and dynamics of international capital markets and flows, the IMF recently established a new International Capital Markets Department. The former managing director of the IMF, Michel Camdessus, was perhaps among the first to emphasize capital-account factors as being the drivers behind recent financial crises in emerging and developing countries in 1995, when he referred to the Mexican crisis of 1994–95 as "the first financial crisis of the twenty-first century" (Buira, 1999, p. 1).

[41] There is a burgeoning literature about the interest-rate impact on exchange rates and capital flows during a crisis period. See, for example, Furman and Stiglitz (1998).

The provision of external financing may, for these reasons, be seen by some as a "public good" and as being appropriately supplied by the IMF.[42] Fischer (2001b) has stressed the need for a multilateral response in the form of IMF lending to complement unilateral measures that countries may take toward liquidity enhancement. This would solve the first-mover problem, whereby no single creditor or investor is ready to extend the first offer of funds to a crisis economy.[43] As noted above, the IMF used to possess a quick-disbursing low-conditionality lending window (the CFF) designed to provide liquidity in the event of trade-related current-account deficits. The trend since the 1980s, however, has been toward greater conditionality, and this, almost by definition, reduces the speed with which liquidity can be disbursed. By the time an IMF program has been negotiated, the internal dynamics of a crisis may be well established and thus more difficult to break. The sheer size of capital movements, compared with budget and trade deficits, may leave the IMF struggling to provide significant financial support, even though the absolute amount of lending to countries encountering capital-account crises may put strains on the IMF's own resources.

One of the problems facing the IMF, and the question constituting one component of the financial-architecture debate has been how to provide adequate liquidity to help forestall and, if needed, help deal with crises where there is reluctance to make concessions in terms of conditionality and reluctance to increase substantially the IMF's lending capacity. The IMF's response has been to create the Contingent Credit Line (CCL). The idea of the CCL was to establish a precautionary line of credit for countries that might be affected by contagion from a crisis and to finance this credit from outside the IMF's quota-based resources by the New Arrangements to Borrow introduced in 1998. The negotiation of conditionality with potential users of the CCL would thus occur before the country needed to draw on the IMF.

---

[42] Of course, another alternative open to individual governments is private lines of credit with international banks. We discuss these in the next subsection.

[43] As Eichengreen (2001b, pp. 24–25) notes,

in the climate of uncertainty that invariably surrounds a crisis, waiting has option value. Investors have an incentive to wait and see whether the commitment to reform is sustained instead of being first to provide new money. New money may increase the likelihood of success—interest rates will come down, making it more likely that growth will resume—but organizing the provision of those funds must surmount the free rider problem in which each investor prefers other investors to be the source of the additional liquidity.

However, no country has negotiated a CCL. Its weaknesses have been widely recognized, and the facility was modified somewhat in late 2000 by reducing the relatively high costs of borrowing from it and by reviewing the conditionality attached to obtaining the funding (Bird, 2001b; Fischer, 2001b; IMF, 2001c; Willett, 2001a).

This sort of tinkering, however, fails to recognize a more fundamental drawback of such a scheme. Why should countries sacrifice any degree of sovereignty over national policy and subject themselves to strict conditionality, when all they receive in return is an option on a drawing? Because countries often fail to implement conditionality for one reason or another, a situation could arise in which a country complies with a significant proportion of conditionality and yet is ineligible to draw once it experiences contagion from a crisis. Of most concern, though, has been the possibility that by negotiating a CCL, a country sends a negative signal to private-capital markets that it is vulnerable to a crisis. The range of *ex ante* conditionality may paint a bleak picture of what is wrong. This may have an adverse effect on capital flows and may contribute to causing the very crisis that the CCL is intended to help prevent. Moreover, there remains some doubt about whether the facility would be adequately financed. Because contagion from crisis has turned out to be more of a regional than a global phenomenon,[44] industrial economies may perceive that they receive few benefits from the CCL and may be reluctant to provide finance for it (Chang and Rajan, 2001).

This raises the question of whether the principle of subsidiarity suggests that a regional system of contingent credit lines should be established that is similar to the bilateral swaps used to support pegged exchange rates during the Bretton Woods era. There are signs that the Asian economies are moving in this direction.

Self-Help Mechanisms in Asia

Unilateral liquidity-enhancing policies. As noted above, economies in Asia have, to some extent, strengthened their international liquidity

---

[44] For instance, in a recent study using a sample of twenty countries covering the periods of the 1982 Mexican debt crisis, the 1994–95 Tequila crisis, and the 1997–98 Asian crisis, De Gregorio and Valdes (2001) find contagion to be directly dependent on *geographical horizon*. Using a panel of annual data for nineteen developing economies for the period from 1977 to 1993, Krueger, Osakwe, and Page (2000) conclude that a currency crisis in a *regional economy* raises the probability of a speculative attack on the domestic currency by about 8.5 percentage points. All of these findings provide a rationale for developing regionally based contingent credit facilities to buttress reserve holdings of individual countries so as to prevent sudden credit contraction caused by a liquidity crisis.

positions by replenishing and accumulating reserves and by lengthening the average maturity of their external indebtedness. This increased liquidity, along with the introduction of relatively greater flexibility in the exchange-rate regimes, may have eased their vulnerability to the destabilizing effects of volatile capital flows.[45] This does not mean, however, that liquidity in the region is now adequate to avoid future crises. Moreover, as the economies of the region continue to recover from the 1997–98 crisis, imports will rise and current-account surpluses will tend to fall; the rate of accumulation of international reserves will consequently also decline. In any case, beyond a certain point, reserve accumulation is likely to be an inefficient way of creating liquidity. Because liquidity may be needed only in certain sets of circumstances, as in the event of sudden outflows of private capital, contingent credit lines may be a better way of trying to deal with the problem. Are there other ways in which contingent credit lines can be established outside the IMF?

Some emerging economies, including Argentina, Indonesia, Mexico, and South Africa, have recently arranged private lines of credit with international banks. There are a number of problems, however, with such privately contracted credit lines (Rajan, 2002c). First, there may be high opportunity costs, insofar as the individual countries have to commit certain assets or revenue streams as collateral. Second, calling on these lines of credit when needed could lead to a hike in the country's international risk premium. Third, while negotiating lines of credit with a country, the financial institutions could undermine the effectiveness of these commitments and their net exposures to that country through other channels (through various techniques of corporate risk management). Foreign banks might themselves transmit crises. In response to a crisis in one country, for example, multinational banks might attempt to liquidate positions in other regional economies either to enhance overall liquidity or to reduce (perceived) portfolio risk. Eichengreen (2001b) discusses the inefficacy of such private CCLs in the context of Argentina's recent experience.[46]

Monetary cooperation. Suffice it to note here that the regional dimension of the 1997–98 financial crisis, as well as the perceived

---

[45] Of course, Malaysia is the exception, having introduced a system of capital controls along with a fixed peg to the U.S. dollar.

[46] The Argentine experience is revealing, because Argentina had often been held up to other emerging and developing countries as a poster child of how to establish good "investor relations" in the 1990s.

inadequacies of the IMF's response to it, have motivated East Asian economies to explore regionally based institutional alternatives. A subgroup of East Asian economies have taken some small but noteworthy steps toward enhancing regional financial stability and protecting themselves against externally induced shocks and liquidity crises. The establishment of the Manila Framework Group, the ASEAN Surveillance Process (which is managed by the newly created ASEAN Surveillance Coordinating Unit), and the recently formed Regional Economic Monitoring Unit of the Asian Development Bank (ADB) are all steps in the right direction. These initiatives have been discussed in some detail by Chang and Rajan (1999, 2001), Rajan (2000), Manzano (2001), and others and will not be repeated here. Although initiatives toward enhanced regional surveillance are important in their own right, they do not guarantee that capital-account crises will be avoided. Access to international credit lines may still be required.

Against this background, and in recognition of the fact that financial stability has the characteristics of a regional public good, it is important to note that selected East Asian economies have recently agreed to create a network of bilateral currency swaps and repurchase agreements (repos) as a "firewall" against future financial crises. This agreement has since come to be termed the "Chiang Mai Initiative" (CMI) following an agreement in Chiang Mai, Thailand, on May 6, 2000.

In broad terms, the CMI is aimed at providing additional short-term hard currencies to countries facing the possibility of a liquidity shortfall. The CMI extends and expands upon the little-known ASEAN Swap Arrangement (ASA) and encompasses all ASEAN countries as well as China, Japan, and Korea (ASEAN + 3). The ASA was established in the 1970s to provide short-term swap facilities to members facing temporary liquidity or balance-of-payments problems. In 1977, there were only five ASEAN signatories—Indonesia, Malaysia, the Philippines, Singapore, and Thailand—each contributing about US $40 million. At the Fourth ASEAN Finance Ministers Meeting in Brunei Darussalam on March 25 and 26, 2000, the ministers agreed to expand the ASA to include the remaining ASEAN members, Brunei Darussalam, Cambodia, the Lao People's Democratic Republic, Myanmar, and Vietnam. In keeping with this expansion, the ASA was enlarged to US $1 billion with effect from November 17, 2000. There are also a series of repurchase agreements that allow ASEAN members with collateral such as U.S. Treasury bills to swap them for hard currency (usually U.S. dollars) and then repurchase them at a later date. The expanded ASA is to be made available for two years and is renewable upon mutual agreement of the members. Each member is allowed to draw a maximum of twice its commitment from the facility for a period of up to six months, with the possibility of a further extension of not more than six months.

This expansion of the ASA is the first step in implementing the CMI. In addition to the expansion of the ASA among Southeast Asian countries, the three ASEAN Dialog partners (China, Japan, and Korea) have simultaneously been in discussions aimed at establishing bilateral swap arrangements (BSAs) among themselves. Japan has recently signed BSAs totaling US $6 billion with Korea, Malaysia, and Thailand and is planning to add swaps with China and the Philippines. Swap arrangements among other members of the ASEAN + 3 group are expected in the near future.[47] The maximum amount of withdrawal under each of the BSAs will be determined by negotiations between the two countries concerned, but the members of the regional partnership plan to coordinate and consult thoroughly among themselves when deciding on disbursements. Although the basic idea behind the CMI is clear, the details must still be explained. Journalistic accounts suggest that 10 percent of the funds will be available automatically, whereas the rest will be subject to IMF conditionality. Other details about the new swap arrangements, such as the kind of collateral that may be required for hard-currency loans, the interest rate that will charged, and the number of withdrawals that can be made, are not yet known. However, economic analysis helps to identify some broad principles that should be included in the initiative. First, the resources must be capable of being disbursed quickly; speed is essential during a crisis. Second, the credit lines must be large enough to generate confidence in private-capital markets and to repel speculative attacks and must involve a sufficient number of countries so as to avoid potential problems of covariance and to allow for the pooling of risks. Nonetheless, it remains an open issue as to what is meant by "large enough," or as Jeanne and Wyplosz (2001) note, "how large is large?"[48] It is unclear whether the

[47] Although Singapore is a contributor to the ASA, it has announced its intention not to sign bilateral swap agreements under the Chiang Mai Initiative at this time.

[48] In the final analysis, a referee notes that
to the extent that capital is free to move and speculators can sell short the domestic currency, the demand for foreign currency is virtually infinite. Would foreign central banks be willing to inflate their money supply without restrictions to prevent a neighbor country from experiencing a crisis? If historical experience is any guide, they would not. At the time of the 1992 ERM crisis, Germany could well have extended credit lines to France, the UK and Italy. It did not. Since no country would agree to an infinite reserve swap, there is a limit to the stabilizing properties of such a scheme.

existing swaps are sufficient to tackle future capital reversals. Indeed, during the Asian crisis of 1997–98, the ASA was not even activated, because the financing levels available through these channels were considered grossly insufficient in the face of the massive capital with-drawals experienced by the regional economies. It is for this reason that one component of monetary regionalism has been an expansion of the scheme to include capital-rich North Asian economies like Japan. Third, the rate of interest needs to be sufficiently high so as to guard against moral hazard, that is, an increased readiness of creditors and debtors to court risk (countries should be discouraged from using such credit lines as a matter of course).[49] Fourth, access to such liquidity should be separated from the detailed negotiation of conditionality, which would prejudice quick dispersal; links to IMF conditionality may be some cause of concern. However, given the part played in the East Asian crisis by weak domestic financial structures, inadequate pruden-tial standards, and supervision, there is a strong argument for making access to CMI credit lines conditional upon compliance with some minimum set of financial standards. This would encourage countries to push ahead with reforms to their domestic financial systems.

A credible system of regional swaps based on these principles would have two key attractions. Not only would it enable participants to avoid the severe output losses that are associated with extreme shortages of liquidity, it would also reduce the incidence of crises by creating confidence that such extreme shortages will not occur. Of course,

---

This suggests that swap lines are likely to be effective only in combination with some form of *ex post* capital controls.

It is interesting to note, in this regard, that the IMF has been fairly supportive of such unilateral actions to restrain international financial flows. For instance, a recent IMF study (Ishii, Otker-Obe, and Cui, 2001, p. 1) has concluded that measures to limit the offshore trading of currencies "could be effective if they were comprehensive and effectively enforced, and were accompanied by consistent macroeconomic policies and structural reform." Following the lead of Singapore, Indonesia and Thailand have taken measures to curb currency speculation by imposing quantitative restrictions on the offshore trading of their respective currencies.

[49] The need to charge "prohibitively high" interest rates is, of course, the classic rule for a lender of last resort proposed by Walter Bagehot. Park (2001a) also discusses the issue of the appropriate interest rate for a regional financial facility. Willett (2001a) suggests that *ex ante* lending facilities should follow a policy of "time escalating interest rates." Admittedly, this does not solve the moral-hazard problem at the creditor or investor level. We thank a referee for pointing this out. The way to limit such investor moral hazard would be for the private sector to share in the burden of bailouts, that is, "take a haircut." We take this point up again in the latter part of this section.

confidence would be undermined if the swap arrangements were used to try to defend disequilibrium real exchange rates, and the CMI should, therefore, not be a mechanism for inappropriate currency pegging in the region. Again, the history of bilateral swaps in the context of the Bretton Woods system demonstrates that they are an ineffective means of defending seriously misaligned currencies.[50]

Park (2001a) and Wang (2002) provide comprehensive descriptions of the CMI and offer useful suggestions about how it might be extended. We note here only that there are at least two additional reasons to believe that regional arrangements to augment international liquidity have a comparative advantage over multilateral arrangements when it comes to providing contingent credit lines. First, regional credit lines would have more of the features of a credit union than the IMF possesses. All participants in them would be able to perceive circumstances in which they might themselves need to use the credit lines, and these vested interests should create a stronger motivation to make the system successful than might exist in the case of the IMF's CCL. Second, prudential and supervisory standards might be more appropriately set at the regional level, where special circumstances could be more easily identified and addressed.

Before proceeding, an important caveat is in order. The focus here has been on providing liquidity. Financial stability almost certainly requires complementary policies such as officially sanctioned standstills, collective-action clauses, and voluntary debt exchanges, along with a "constructive engagement" among creditors, debtors, and regional and international financial institutions. As Willett (2001a, p. 12) notes,

> it is true that the provision of a LOLR is not the only way to deal with a liquidity crisis. Payments stand stills and other forms of private sector

---

[50] We should note that the Asian and Pacific region already has a financial cooperative scheme in place in the form of the Executives' Meeting of East Asia-Pacific Central Banks (EMEAP). The EMEAP is a cooperative organization comprising central banks and monetary authorities of eleven economies: Australia, China, Hong Kong, Indonesia, Japan, Korea, Malaysia, New Zealand, the Philippines, Singapore, and Thailand. Spurred on by the Tequila crisis of 1994–95, EMEAP has taken substantive steps toward monetary cooperation. For instance, a number of member economies signed a series of bilateral repurchase agreements in 1995 and 1996. Hong Kong and Singapore also reached an agreement to intervene in foreign-exchange markets on behalf of the Bank of Japan. These creditor regional economies also tried to defend the Thai baht for some period before the Bank of Thailand succumbed to the speculative pressures (Rajan, 2000). There seems to have been no discussion in policy circles about the nexus between the EMEAP scheme and the CMI.

involvement (PSI) are also possible. Indeed many international monetary experts believe that such measures are likely to be a part of any efficient reform of the international financial architecture. I agree with this analysis, but would emphasize that such measures are likely to be only a complement not a full substitute for a LOLR. Developments on PSI should of course influence the size of loans from a LOLR.[51]

Regionalism and Multilateralism in the Architecture Debate

If the Chiang Mai Initiative is to be expanded as a way of providing short-term liquidity at the regional level, it is natural to ask to what extent this will define an agenda for an Asian monetary fund (AMF). A successful introduction of a network of regional swap arrangements in East Asia (possibly enlarged over time to encompass most of Asia, as defined by the ADB) has been viewed by some observers as an important step toward the eventual creation of a full-fledged regional monetary facility (Ariff, 2001; Rowley, 2001; Wang, 2002).

Although early proposals for an AMF, coming from the Japanese government in September 1997, were opposed strongly by the United States and appeared to have been dropped, the proposal reemerged at the East Asian Summit organized by the World Economic Forum in Singapore in October 1999. In November 1999, ASEAN ministers discussed the idea at an informal summit in the Philippines (Manila). A view that little progress has been achieved in reforming the international financial architecture has further reignited the debate about an AMF. The precise form that an AMF would take, however, varies across the specific proposals. The original Japanese proposal envisaged its role as being one of making available a pool of funds that would be disbursed quickly to provide emergency balance-of-payments support to countries in crisis. A related proposal by Malaysian prime minister Mahathir Mohamad envisages a wider role. In his proposal, an AMF would be a "a small compact wholly regional funding organisation which would be deeply and constantly engaged in East Asian monetary co-operation and problems on a daily basis" (World Economic Forum Press Release, October 19, 1999). The IMF's managing director, Horst Köhler (2001), has expressed support for regional initiatives as long as they do not compete with the IMF.

---

[51] Indeed, referring to the CMI initiatives, a referee has also commented that "without standstill or bond covenants, it is difficult to see how this proposal could improve financial stability." Similarly, Eichengreen (2001b) and the IMF (2001c) discuss in some detail the role of the private sector in resolving financial crises (also see references cited by Willett, 2001a, p. 12).

48

So, would a new Asian financial architecture, perhaps based on an AMF, threaten or facilitate international financial stability? Would regional reform be a stepping-stone or a stumbling bloc to international monetary reform? It could be a stumbling bloc if loans from the AMF carried conditionality that was inconsistent with that coming from the IMF. Moreover, the attitude among the industrial economies that Asia is looking after its own problems could reduce the urgency with which reform at the international level is pursued. Accordingly, it is important to identify the comparative advantages of regional and international financial institutions and the division of labor between them.

Boughton (1997, p. 3) has reminded us that "although the intention was that the availability of the Fund's resources should prevent countries from experiencing financial crisis, in practice, the institution has often found itself helping its members cope with crises after they occur." Reforms that allow the IMF to bolster its lending capacity significantly through quota increases or direct borrowing from private-capital markets may be unlikely (Bird and Rowlands, 2001). Monetary and financial regionalism is consistent with the principle of "subsidiarity" and could help the IMF fulfill its stated aim. Why choose to deal with a problem at the global level when it can be handled adequately and perhaps more effectively at the regional level? Just as multilateral trade liberalization and multilateral trade institutions have been joined by an increasing array of regional trading arrangements, regional financial crises may be better handled by regional arrangements. To the extent that regional arrangements may help reinvigorate interests in strengthening the international financial architecture, they could act as "stepping stones" toward multilateral reforms (Park, 2001a, makes a similar argument). Regional arrangements ought to promote greater commitment to, and national ownership of, programs and conditionality, a point that is universally recognized as being of significant importance.

Things could be organized along the following lines. On the basis of work done by the Basle Committee, an AMF could stipulate financial standards appropriate to an Asian context. Asian countries could commit themselves to achieve these standards over a specified period of time. Being on course in terms of meeting these standards could then be a precondition for financial support from the AMF in the event of contagion from a regional crisis. Loans from the AMF would carry nothing equivalent to IMF conditionality and would be available only on a short-term basis and at a high interest rate to help avoid potential moral-hazard problems. The very existence of additional short-term liquidity could reduce the incidence of speculation and crisis. Countries

49

with fundamental and longer-term economic problems would still have to turn to the IMF, where they would be exposed to IMF conditionality. By providing an extra incentive for members to reform their domestic financial systems, a process that may not yet have gone far enough, the AMF could help to prevent future crises. By providing an additional source of short-term liquidity, it could take financial pressure off the IMF during crisis periods. The IMF would continue to stand ready to assist economies where regional arrangements failed to resolve problems, but should this occur, it might be more reasonable to assume that these problems were not exclusively caused by shortages of liquidity, and this would raise the credibility of IMF conditionality. Elaborating on the issue, Park (2001a, p. 6) notes that

> there is also the argument that regional financial management could be structured and managed to be complementary to the role of the IMF. For example, an East Asian regional fund could provide additional resources to the IMF while joining forces to work on matters related to the prevention and management of financial crises. An East Asian monetary fund could also support the work of the IMF by monitoring economic developments in the region and taking part in the IMF's global surveillance activities. The East Asian monetary fund could also be designed initially as a regional lender of the last resort while the IMF assumes the role of prescribing macroeconomic policies to the member countries of the East Asian monetary fund.

Beyond cooperation with regard to surveillance, the AMF could work closely with the IMF to develop Asia-appropriate mechanisms to involve the private sector in crisis resolution and to promote "constructive engagement" and constant dialog among creditors and debtors, as, for example, through EMEAP (see n. 50). In this way, an AMF could contribute to enhanced international financial stability.

6 Concluding Remarks

Although the debate about a new international financial architecture was launched before the East Asian crisis of 1997–98, much of the pressure for a new architecture derived from that crisis. Progress toward restructuring has been slow, piecemeal, and largely cosmetic, however. The fact that contagion from the crisis was regionally contained has reduced the motivation for reform at the global level, and with the debate winding down, the chances of deep and meaningful global reform are small. Within the Asian region, however, the outlook may be different. It is the Asian economies that have experienced the ongoing costs of crisis and contagion. Moreover, Japan, the dominant

50

regional power, remains trapped in the economic doldrums. There may thus be significant motivation for reform at the regional level.

Although dollarization may be inappropriate for Asian economies, and talk of a regional currency union along European lines is, at the very least, premature, there is certainly scope for closer regional financial cooperation. A reformed Asian financial architecture could include the coordination of reforms to domestic financial systems, exchange-rate policies, and short-term contingency lending. An Asian monetary fund could provide the organizational framework within which cooperation could be orchestrated.

Far from prejudicing international reform, which has a low probability of implementation, or of competing with the IMF, a reformed Asian financial architecture could enhance global financial stability by helping to clarify the role of the IMF and by reducing the constraints on resources that the IMF sometimes encounters. It could diminish the need for the IMF to provide contingency credit lines—an area in which it has been, and is likely to remain, unsuccessful—and could ameliorate the criticism that the IMF has opted for excessive conditionality, responding to liquidity crises by requiring substantial adjustment. The historical evidence is that as countries develop, they eventually graduate away from the IMF. This is true of both the United States and the members of the European Union, even the less rich ones. It may be that in the foreseeable future, the move toward greater financial self-reliance in Asia is a fairly natural evolution that should be actively encouraged by the global community.

References

Adler, Michael, "Exchange Rate Planning for the International Trading Firm," in Yakov Amihud and Richard M. Levich, eds., *Exchange Rates and Corporate Performance*, New York, Irwin, 1996, pp. 165–180.

Ariff, Mohamed, "The Asian Monetary Fund: Is East Asia Ready?" paper presented at the Malaysian Institute of Economic Research Conference on the National Economic Outlook 2002, Kuala Lumpur, November 6–7, 2001.

Asian Development Bank (ADB), *Asian Development Outlook 2000*, Manila, Oxford University Press, 2000.

Asian Development Bank–Asia Recovery Information Centre (ADB-ARIC), *Asia Recovery Report*, October 2000; March 2001a; June 2001b; available at www.aric.adb.org.

Athukorala, Prema Chandra, *Crisis and Recovery in Malaysia: The Role of Capital Control*, Cheltenham, Elgar, 2001.

Berg, Andrew, and Eduardo R. Borenzstein, "The Pros and Cons of Full Dollarization, International Monetary Fund Working Paper No. 50/00, Washington, D.C., International Monetary Fund, March 2000.

Bird, Graham, "Is Dollarisation a Viable Option for Latin America?" *World Economics*, 2 (January-March 2001a), pp. 137–147.

——, "Restructuring the IMF's Lending Facilities," Surrey Centre for International Economic Studies, University of Surrey, June 2001b, processed.

——, "Where Do We Stand On Choosing Exchange Rate Regimes in Developing and Emerging Economies?" *World Economics*, 3 (forthcoming 2002).

Bird, Graham, and Ramkishen S. Rajan, "All at SEA: Exchange Rate Policy in Developing Countries After Nominal Anchors," Surrey Centre for International Economic Studies, University of Surrey, August 2000a, processed.

——, "Is There a Case for an Asian Monetary Fund?" *World Economics*, 1 (April-June 2000b), pp. 135–143.

——, "Recovery or Recession? Post-Devaluation Output Collapse: The Thai Experience," Discussion Paper No. 0043, Centre for International Economic Studies, University of Adelaide, November 2000c.

——, "Banks, Financial Liberalisation and Financial Crises in Emerging Markets," *World Economy*, 24 (July 2001a), pp. 889–910.

——, "Coping with, and Cashing in on, Capital Volatility," *Journal of International Development*, 13 (May 2001b), pp. 1–23.

——, "International Currency Taxation and Currency Stabilisation in Developing Countries," *Journal of Development Studies*, 37 (February 2001c), pp. 21–38.

Bird, Graham, and Dane Rowlands, "Catalysis or Direct Borrowing: The Role of the IMF in Mobilising Private Capital," *World Economy*, 24 (January 2001). pp. 81–98.

Boorman, Jack, Timothy Lane, Marianne Schulze-Ghattas, Ales Bulir, Atish R. Ghosh, Javier Hamann, Alexandros Mourmouras, and Steven Phillips, "Managing Financial Crises—The Experience in East Asia," International Monetary Fund Working Paper No. 00/107, Washington, D.C., International Monetary Fund, June 2000.

Boughton, James M., "From Suez to Tequila: The Fund as Crisis Manager," International Monetary Fund Working Paper No. 97/90, Washington, D.C., International Monetary Fund, July 1997.

Buira, Ariel, *An Alternative Approach to Financial Crises*, Essays in International Finance No. 212, Princeton, N.J., Princeton University, International Finance Section, February 1999.

Bussière, Matthieu, and Christian Mulder, "External Vulnerability in Emerging Market Economies: How High Liquidity Can Offset Weak Fundamentals and the Effects of Contagion," International Monetary Fund Working Paper No. 99/88, Washington, D.C., International Monetary Fund, July 1999.

Calvo, Guillermo, "Fixed versus Flexible Exchange Rates: Preliminaries of a Turn-of-Millennium Rematch," Department of Economics, University of Maryland, May 1999, processed.

Calvo, Guillermo, and Carmen Reinhart, "Fixing for Your Life," in Susan M. Collins and Dani Rodrik, eds., *Brookings Trade Forum 2000: Policy Challenges in the Next Millennium*, Washington, D.C., Brookings Institution, 2000, pp. 1–57.

———, "Fear of Floating," National Bureau of Economic Research Working Paper No. 7993, Cambridge, Mass., National Bureau of Economic Research, November 2001.

Chang, Li Lin, and Ramkishen S. Rajan, "East Asian Cooperation in Light of the Regional Crises: A Case of Self-Help or No-Help?" *Australian Journal of International Affairs*, 53 (April 1999), pp. 261–281.

———, "The Economics and Politics of Monetary Regionalism in Asia," *ASEAN Economic Bulletin*, 18 (April 2001), pp. 103–118.

Chang, Roberto, and Andrés Velasco, "The Asian Liquidity Crisis," National Bureau of Economic Research Working Paper No. 6796, Cambridge, Mass., National Bureau of Economic Research, November 1998.

Claessens, Stijn, Asli Demirgüç-Kunt, and Harry Huizinga, "How Does Foreign Entry Affect Domestic Banking Markets?" World Bank Policy Research Working Paper No. 1918, Washington, D.C., World Bank, June 1998.

Claessens, Stijn, Simeon Djankov, and Daniela Klingebiel, "Financial Restructuring in East Asia: Halfway There?" Financial Sector Discussion Paper No. 3, Washington, D.C., World Bank, September 1999.

Claessens, Stijn, and Tom Glaessner, "Internationalization of Financial Services in Asia," World Bank Policy Research Working Paper No. 1911, Washington, D.C., World Bank, April 1998.

Corbo, Vittorio, and Michael W. Cox, "Exchange Rate Volatility, Investment and Growth: Some New Evidence," in William C. Gruben, David M. Gould, and Carlos E. Zarazaga, eds., *Exchange Rates, Capital Flows, and Monetary Policy in a Changing World Economy*, Proceedings of a Conference of the Federal Reserve Bank of Dallas, September 14–15, 1995, Boston, Dordrecht, and London, Kluwer, 1997.

Culp, Christopher L., Steve H. Hanke, and Merton H. Miller, "The Case for an Indonesian Currency Board," *Journal of Applied Corporate Finance*, 11 (Winter 1999), pp. 57–65.

Dadush, Uri, Dipak Dasgupta, and Dilip Ratha, "The Role of Short-Term Debt in Recent Crises," *Finance and Development*, 37 (December 2000), pp. 54–57.

De Gregorio, José, and Rodrigo O. Valdes, "Crisis Transmission: Evidence from the Debt, Tequila, and Asian Flu Crises," *World Bank Economic Review*, 15 (No. 2, 2001), pp. 289–314.

Disyatat, Piti, "Currency Crises and Foreign Reserves—A Simple Model," International Monetary Fund Working Paper No. 01/18, Washington, D.C., International Monetary Fund, February 2001.

Edwards, Sebastian, "Exchange Rates as Nominal Anchors," *Weltwirtschaftliches Archiv*, 129 (1993), pp. 1–32.

Eichengreen, Barry, "Can Emerging Markets Float? Should They Inflation Target?" Department of Economics, University of California at Berkeley, April 2001a, processed.

———, "Crisis Prevention and Management: Any New Lessons from Argentina and Turkey?" Department of Economics, University of California at Berkeley, October 2001b, processed.

———, "When to Dollarize?" *Journal of Money, Credit and Banking*, 34 (forthcoming 2002).

Eichengreen, Barry, and Tamim Bayoumi, "Is Asia an Optimum Currency Area? Can It Become One? Regional, Global, and Historical Perspectives on Asian Monetary Relations," in Stefan Collignon, Jean Pisani-Ferry, and Yung Chul Park, eds., *Exchange Rate Policies in Emerging Asian Countries*, Routledge Studies in the Growth Economies of Asia, Vol. 13, London and New York, Routledge, 1999a, pp. 347–366.

———, "On Regional Monetary Arrangements for ASEAN," paper presented at the International Conference on Exchange Rate Regimes in Emerging Market Economies, Tokyo, December 17–18, 1999b.

Eichengreen, Barry, and Harold James, "Monetary and Financial Reform in Two Eras of Globalization (and in between)," Department of Economics, University of California at Berkeley, April 2001, processed.

Eichengreen, Barry, and Donald J. Mathieson, "The Currency Composition of Foreign Exchange Reserves: Retrospect and Prospect," International Monetary Fund Working Paper No. 00/131, Washington, D.C., International Monetary Fund, July 2000.

Eichengreen, Barry, and Andrew K. Rose, "To Defend or Not to Defend? That is the Question," Department of Economics, University of California at Berkeley, February 2001, processed.

Felix, David, "Financial Globalization versus Free Trade: The Case for the Tobin Tax," *UNCTAD Review* (1996), pp. 63–103.

Felix, David, and Ranjit Sau, "On the Revenue Potential and Phasing In of the Tobin Tax," in Mahbub ul Haq, Inge Kaul, and Isabelle Grunberg, eds., *The Tobin Tax: Coping with Financial Volatility*, New York and Oxford, Oxford University Press, 1996, pp. 223–254.

Fischer, Stanley, "Opening Remarks," IMF/World Bank International Reserves: Policy Issues Forum, Washington, D.C., April 28, 2001a.

———, "Reducing Vulnerabilities: The Role of the Contingent Credit Line," paper presented at the Inter-American Development Bank, Washington, D.C., April 25, 2001b.

Frankel, Jeffrey A., "The International Financial Architecture," *Policy Brief* No. 51, Washington D.C., Brookings Institution, June 1999.

Frankel, Jeffrey A., and Andrew K. Rose, "The Endogeneity of the Optimum Currency Area Criteria," *Economic Journal*, 108 (July 1998), pp. 1009–1025.

———, "Estimating the Effect of Currency Unions on Trade and Output," National Bureau of Economic Research Working Paper No. 7857, Cambridge, Mass., National Bureau of Economic Research, August 2000.

Frankel, Jeffrey, Sergio L. Schmukler, and Luis Servén, "Verifiability and the Vanishing Intermediate Exchange Rate Regime," in Susan M. Collins and Dani Rodrik, eds., *Brookings Trade Forum 2000: Policy Challenges in the Next Millennium*, Washington, D.C., Brookings Institution, 2000, pp. 59–108.

Frankel, Jeffrey, and Shang-Jin Wei, "Yen Bloc or Dollar Bloc: Exchange Rate Policies of the East Asian Economies," in Takatoshi Ito and Anne O. Krueger, eds., *Macroeconomic Linkage: Savings, Exchange Rates, and Capital Flows*, NBER-East Asia Seminar on Economics, Vol. 3, Chicago and London, University of Chicago Press, 1994, pp. 295–329.

Friberg, Richard, and Anders Vredin, "Exchange Rate Uncertainty and the Microeconomic Benefits from EMU," *Swedish Economic Policy Review*, 4 (Autumn 1997), pp. 547–594.

Furman, Jason, and Joseph E. Stiglitz, "Economic Crises: Evidence and Insights from East Asia," *Brookings Papers on Economic Activity*, No. 2 (1998), pp. 1–114.

Gavin, Michael, and Roberto Perotti, "Fiscal Policy in Latin America," *NBER Macroeconomics Annual 1997*, Cambridge, Mass., and London, MIT Press, 1997, pp. 11–61.

Ghosh, Atish R., Anne-Marie Gulde, Jonathan Ostry, and Holger C. Wolf, "Does the Nominal Exchange Rate Regime Matter?" International Monetary Fund Working Paper No. 95/121, Washington, D.C., International Monetary Fund, November 1995.

Glick, Reuven, Michael Hutchison, and Ramon Moreno, "Is Pegging the Exchange Rate a Cure for Inflation?" in Richard J. Sweeney, Clas G. Wihlborg, and Thomas D. Willett, eds., *Exchange-Rate Policies for Emerging Market Economies*, Political Economy of Global Interdependence Series, Boulder, Colo., and Oxford, Westview, 1999, pp. 165–192.

Glick, Reuven, and Andrew K. Rose, "Does a Currency Union Affect Trade? The Time Series Evidence," National Bureau of Economic Research Working Paper No. 8396, Cambridge, Mass., National Bureau of Economic Research, July 2001.

Goodhart, Charles A. E., "The Political Economy of Monetary Union," in Peter B. Kenen, ed., *Understanding Interdependence: The Macroeconomics of the Open Economy*, Princeton, N.J., Princeton University Press, 1995, pp. 448–505.

Grenville, Stephen, and David Gruen, "Capital Flows and Exchange Rates" Sydney, Reserve Bank of Australia, Research Department, August 1999, processed.

Haque, Nadeem Ul, Manmohan S. Kumar, Mark Nelson, and Donald J. Mathieson, "The Economic Content of Indicators of Developing Country Creditworthiness," *International Monetary Fund Staff Papers*, 43 (December 1996), pp. 688–724.

Hausmann, Ricardo, "Should There Be Five Currencies or One Hundred and Five?" *Foreign Policy*, 116 (Fall 1999), pp. 65–79.

Hausmann, Ricardo, Ugo Panizza, and Ernesto Stein, "Why Do Countries Float the Way They Float?" *Journal of Development Economics*, 66 (December 2001), pp. 387–414.

Hernandez, Leonardo F., and Peter J. Montiel, "Post-Crisis Exchange Rate Policy in Five Asian Countries: Filling in the 'Hollow Middle'" International Monetary Fund Working Paper No. 01/170, Washington, D.C., International Monetary Fund, November 2001.

Hills, Carla, Peter Peterson, and Martin Goldstein, "Safeguarding Prosperity in a Global Financial System: The Future of International Financial Architecture," Report of an Independent Task Force Sponsored by the Council on Foreign Relations, New York, Council on Foreign Relations, 1999.

Honohan, Patrick, and Daniela Klingebiel, "Controlling Fiscal Costs of Banking Crises," World Bank Policy Research Working Paper No. 2441, Washington, D.C., World Bank, September 2000.

Huizinga, John, "Exchange Rate Volatility, Uncertainty, and Investment: An Empirical Investigation," in Leonardo Leiderman and Assaf Razin, eds., *Capital Mobility: The Impact on Consumption, Investment and Growth*, Cambridge, New York, and Melbourne, Cambridge University Press, 1994, pp. 185–213.

International Monetary Fund (IMF), *World Economic Outlook*, Washington, D.C. International Monetary Fund, 1997; 2000.

———, *International Capital Markets: Development, Prospects and Key Policy Issues*, Washington, D.C. International Monetary Fund, September 1999.

———, *Annual Report 2001*, Washington, D.C., International Monetary Fund, September 2001a.

———, "Reforming the International Financial Architecture," Issues Brief 01/01, Washington, D.C., International Monetary Fund, March 9, 2001b.

———, "Resolving and Preventing Financial Crises: The Role of the Private Sector," Issues Brief 01/02, Washington, D.C., International Monetary Fund, March 26, 2001c.

Ishii, Shogo, Inci Otker-Obe, and Li Cui, "Measures to Limit the Offshore Use of Currencies—Pros and Cons," International Monetary Fund Working Paper No. 01/43, Washington, D.C., International Monetary Fund, April 2001.

Jeanne, Olivier, "Foreign Currency Debt and the Global Financial Architecture," *European Economic Review*, 44 (May 2000), pp. 719–727.

Jeanne, Olivier, and Charles Wyplosz, "The International Lender of Last Resort: How Large is Large Enough?" International Monetary Fund Working Paper No. 01/76, Washington, D.C., International Monetary Fund, May 2001.

Kaplan, Ethan, and Dani Rodrik, "Did the Malaysian Capital Controls Work?" National Bureau of Economic Research Working Paper No. 8142, Cambridge, Mass., National Bureau of Economic Research, February 2001.

Kawaii, Masahiro, "Bank and Corporate Restructuring in Crisis-Affected East Asia: From Systematic Collapse to Reconstruction," in Gordon de Brouwer, ed., *Financial Markets and Policies in East Asia*, London, Routledge, 2002, pp. 82–121.

Kenen, Peter B., "Currency Areas, Policy Domains, and the Institutionalization of Fixed Exchange Rates," Discussion Paper No. 467, Centre for
Economic Performance, London School of Economics, August, 2000.

——, *The International Financial Architecture: What's New? What's Miss-
ing?* Washington, D.C., Institute for International Economics, 2001.

Kim, Tae-Joon, and Jai-Won Ryou, "The Optimal Currency Basket and the
Currency Bloc in Asia," *Bank of Korea Economic Papers*, 4 (May 2001), pp.
194–216.

Klingebiel, Daniela, "The Use of Asset Management Companies in the Resolution of Banking Crises: Cross-Country Experiences," Washington, D.C.,
World Bank, October 1999, processed.

Köhler, Horst, "New Challenges for Exchange Rate Policy," paper presented
at the Asia-Europe Meeting of Finance Ministers, Kobe, January 13, 2001.

Krueger, Mark, Patrick N. Osakwe, and Jennifer Page, "Fundamentals, Contagion and Currency Crises: An Empirical Analysis," *Development Policy
Review*, 18 (September 2000), pp. 257–274.

Krugman, Paul, "Balance Sheets, The Transfer Problem, and Financial Crisis,"
in Peter Isard, Assaf Razin, and Andrew K. Rose, eds., *International
Finance and Financial Crises: Essays in Honor of Robert P. Flood, Jr.*,
Boston, Dordrecht, London, Kluwer, 1999, pp. 31–45.

Kwan, Chi Hung, *Enken no Keizaigaku (The Economics of the Yen Bloc)*,
Tokyo, Nihon Keiza Shinbunsha, 1995.

Lane, Timothy, Atish Ghosh, Javier Hamann, Steven Phillips, Marianne
Schulze-Ghattas, and Tsidi Tsikata, *IMF-Supported Programs in Indonesia,
Korea, and Thailand: A Preliminary Assessment*, Occasional Paper No. 178,
Washington, D.C., International Monetary Fund, June 1999.

Levine, Ross, "Foreign Banks, Financial Development, and Economic
Growth," in Claude E. Barfield, ed., *International Financial Markets:
Harmonization versus Competition*, Washington, D.C., AEI Press, 1996.

Lindgren, Carl-Johan, Tomás J. T. Baliño, Charles Enoch, Anne-Marie Gulde,
Marc Quintyn, and Leslie Teo, *Financial Sector Crisis and Restructuring:
Lessons From Asia*, Occasional Paper No. 188, Washington, D.C., Inter-
national Monetary Fund, January 2000.

McKenzie, Michael D., "The Impact of Exchange Rate Volatility on International
Trade Flows," *Journal of Economic Surveys*, 13 (February 1999), pp. 71–103.

McKinnon, Ronald, "The East Asian Dollar Standard, Life After Death,"
Economic Notes, 29 (February 2001), pp. 31–82.

McLean, Ben, and Sona Shrestha (2001), "International Borrowing in Domestic Currency: What Does it Take?" Sydney, Reserve Bank of Australia,
Research Department, 2001, processed.

Manzano, George, "Is There Any Value-Added in the ASEAN Surveillance
Process?" *ASEAN Economic Bulletin*, 18 (April 2001), pp. 94–102.

Mattoo, Aaditya, "Financial Services and the WTO: Liberalisation Commitments of the Developing and Transition Economies," *World Economy*, 23
(February 2000), pp. 351–386.

Meltzer, Allan H., Chairman, "Report of the International Financial Institution Advisory Commission," Washington, D.C., International Financial Institution Advisory Commission, March 2000 (http://phantom-x.gsia.cmu.edu/IFIAC).

Min, Hong G., and Judith A. McDonald, "Does a Thin Foreign Exchange Market Lead to Destabilizing Capital-Market Speculations in the Asian Crisis Countries?" World Bank Policy Research Working Paper No. 2056, Washington, D.C., World Bank, February 1999.

Mishkin, Frederic S., "Prudential Supervision: Why Is It Important and What Are the Issues?" National Bureau of Economic Research Working Paper No. 7926, Cambridge, Mass., National Bureau of Economic Research, September 2000.

Montiel, Peter J., "Policy Responses to Volatile Capital Flows," Department of Economics, Williams College, March 1999, processed.

Montreevat, Sakulrat, and Ramkishen S. Rajan, "Banking Crisis, Restructuring and Liberalization in Emerging Economies: A Case Study of Thailand," Discussion Paper No. 0131, Centre for International Economic Studies, University of Adelaide, June 2001.

Mussa, Michael, Paul R. Masson, Alexander K. Swoboda, Esteban Jadresic, Paolo Mauro, and Andrew Berg, Exchange Rate Regimes in an Increasingly Integrated World Economy, Washington, D.C., International Monetary Fund, 2000.

Nilsson, Kristian, and Lars Nilsson, "Exchange Rate Regimes and Export Performance of Developing Countries," World Economy, 23 (February 2000), pp. 331–349.

Park, Yung Chul, "Beyond the Chiang Mai Initiative: Rationale and Need for a Regional Monetary Arrangement in East Asia," Department of Economics, Korea University, June 2001a, processed.

———, The East Asian Dilemma: Restructuring Out or Growing Out? Essays in International Economics No. 223, Princeton, N.J., Princeton University, International Economics Section, August 2001b.

Rajan, Ramkishen S., "The Japanese Economy and Economic Policy in Light of the East Asian Crisis," Working Paper No. 2, Singapore, Institute of Policy Studies, August 1998.

———, "Financial and Macroeconomic Cooperation in ASEAN: Issues and Policy Initiatives," in Mya Than, ed., ASEAN Beyond the Regional Crisis: Challenges and Initiatives, Singapore, Institute of Southeast Asian Studies, 2000, pp. 126–147.

———, (Ir)relevance of Currency-Crisis Theory to the Devaluation and Collapse of the Thai Baht, Princeton Studies in International Economics No. 88, Princeton, N.J., Princeton University, International Economics Section, February 2001.

———, "Argentina and East Asia: The Peg Does It Yet Again," Economic and Political Weekly, 37 (January 27, 2002a), pp. 116–117.

———, "Exchange Rate Policy Options for Post-Crisis Southeast Asia: Is There a Case for Currency Baskets?" World Economy, 25 (January 2002b), pp. 137–163.

———, "Safeguarding against Capital Account Crises: Unilateral, Regional and Multilateral Options for East Asia," in Gordon de Brouwer, ed., *Financial Arrangements in East Asia*, London, Routledge, forthcoming 2002c.

Rajan, Ramkishen S., Rahul Sen, and Reza Sirega, "Misalignment of the Baht, Trade Imbalances, and the Crisis in Thailand," Discussion Paper No. 0045, Centre for International Economic Studies, University of Adelaide, November 2000.

———, "Hong Kong, Singapore and the East Asian Crisis: How Important Were Trade Spillovers?" *World Economy*, 25 (forthcoming 2002).

Rajan, Ramkishen S., and Chung-Hua Shen, "Are Crisis-Induced Devaluations Contractionary?" Discussion Paper No. 0135, Centre for International Economic Studies, University of Adelaide, September 2001.

Rajan, Ramkishen S., and Reza Siregar, "The Vanishing Intermediate Regime and the Tale of Two Cities: Singapore versus Hong Kong," Discussion Paper No. 0031, Centre for International Economic Studies, University of Adelaide, July 2000.

———, "Private Capital Flows in East Asia: Boom, Bust and Beyond," in Gordon de Brouwer, ed., *Financial Markets and Policies in East Asia*, London, Routledge, 2002, pp. 47–81.

Rockoff, Hugh, "How Long Did It Take the United States to Become an Optimal Currency Area?" National Bureau of Economic Research Working Paper (Historical) No. 0124, Cambridge, Mass., National Bureau of Economic Research, April 2000.

Rodrik, Dani, and Andrés Velasco, "Short-Term Capital Flows," National Bureau of Economic Research Working Paper No. 7364, Cambridge, Mass., National Bureau of Economic Research, September 1999.

Servén, Luis, "Uncertainty, Instability, and Irreversible Investment: Theory, Evidence, and Lessons for Africa," World Bank Policy Research Working Paper No. 1722, Washington, D.C., World Bank, February 1997.

Sonakul, Chatu Mongol, Comments presented at the ADB Conference on Government Bond Market and Financial Sector Development in Developing Asian Economies, Manila, March 28–30, 2000.

Spiegel, Mark M., "A Currency Board for Indonesia?" Economic Letter 98–09, Federal Reserve Bank of San Francisco, March 20, 1998.

Tornell, Aaron, and Andrés Velasco, "Fixed versus Flexible Rates: Which Provides More Fiscal Discipline?" *Journal of Monetary Economics*, 45 (April 2000), pp. 399–436.

Wang, Yunjong, "Instruments and Techniques for Financial Cooperation," in Gordon de Brouwer, ed., *Financial Arrangements in East Asia*, London, Routledge, forthcoming 2002.

Wei, Shang-Jin, "Currency Hedging and Goods Trade," *European Economic Review*, 43 (June 1999), pp. 1371–1394.

Willett, Thomas D., "Exchange Rate Volatility, International Trade, and Resource Allocation: A Perspective on Recent Research," *Journal of International Money and Finance*, 5, Supplement (March 1986), pp. s101–s112.

————, "Restructuring IMF Facilities to Separate Lender of Last Resort and Conditionality Programs: The Meltzer Commission Recommendations as Complements rather than Substitutes," Working Papers in Economics No. 28, Department of Economics, Claremont Graduate University, August 2001a.

————, "Truth in Advertising and the Great Dollarization Scam," *Journal of Policy Modeling*, 23 (April 2001b), pp. 279–289.

Williamson, John, "The Case for a Common Basket Peg for East Asian Currencies," in Stefan Collignon, Jean Pisani-Ferry, and Yung Chul Park, eds., *Exchange Rate Policies in Emerging Asian Countries*, Routledge Studies in the Growth Economies of Asia, Vol. 13, London and New York, Routledge, 1999a, pp. 327–343.

————, "Crawling Bands or Monitoring Bands: How to Manage Exchange Rates in a World of Capital Mobility," *International Economics Policy Briefs*, No. 99–3, Washington, D.C., World Bank, February 1999b.

World Bank, *Global Development Finance*, New York, Oxford University Press, 1999; 2000a.

————, *East Asia Recovery and Beyond*, New York, Oxford University Press, 2000b.

PUBLICATIONS OF THE
INTERNATIONAL ECONOMICS SECTION

Notice to Contributors

The International Economics Section publishes papers in two series. ESSAYS IN INTERNATIONAL ECONOMICS and PRINCETON STUDIES IN INTERNATIONAL ECONOMICS. Two earlier series, REPRINTS IN INTERNATIONAL FINANCE and SPECIAL PAPERS IN INTERNATIONAL ECONOMICS, have been discontinued, with the SPECIAL PAPERS being absorbed into the STUDIES series.

The Section welcomes the submission of manuscripts focused on topics in international trade, international macroeconomics, or international finance. Submissions should address systemic issues for the global economy or, if concentrating on particular economies, should adopt a comparative perspective.

ESSAYS IN INTERNATIONAL ECONOMICS are meant to disseminate new views about international economic events and policy issues. They should be accessible to a broad audience of professional economists.

PRINCETON STUDIES IN INTERNATIONAL ECONOMICS are devoted to new research in international economics or to synthetic treatments of a body of literature. They should be comparable in originality and technical proficiency to papers published in leading economic journals. Papers that are longer and more complete than those publishable in the professional journals are welcome.

Manuscripts should be submitted in triplicate, typed single sided and double spaced throughout on 8½ by 11 white bond paper. Publication can be expedited if manuscripts are computer keyboarded in WordPerfect or a compatible program. Additional instructions and a style guide are available from the Section or on the website at www.princeton.edu/~ies.

How to Obtain Publications

The Section's publications are distributed free of charge to college, university, and public libraries and to nongovernmental, nonprofit research institutions. Eligible institutions may ask to be placed on the Section's permanent mailing list.

Individuals and institutions not qualifying for free distribution may receive all publications for the calendar year for a subscription fee of $45.00. Late subscribers will receive all back issues for the year during which they subscribe.

Publications may be ordered individually, with payment made in advance. All publications (ESSAYS, STUDIES, SPECIAL PAPERS, and REPRINTS) cost $10.00 each; an additional $1.50 should be sent for postage and handling within the United States, Canada, and Mexico; $4 should be added for surface delivery outside the region.

All payments must be made in U.S. dollars. Subscription fees and charges for single issues will be waived for organizations and individuals in countries where foreign-exchange regulations prohibit dollar payments.

Information about the Section and its publishing program is available on the Section's website at www.princeton.edu/~ies. A subscription and order form is printed at the end of this volume. Correspondence should be addressed to:

International Economics Section
Department of Economics, Fisher Hall
Princeton University
Princeton, New Jersey 08544-1021
Tel: 609-258-4048 • Fax: 609-258-1374
E-mail: ies@princeton.edu

List of Recent Publications

A complete list of publications is available at the International Economics Section website at www.princeton.edu/~ies.

ESSAYS IN INTERNATIONAL ECONOMICS
(formerly Essays in International Finance)

186. Alessandro Giustiniani, Francesco Papadia, and Daniela Porciani, *Growth and Catch-Up in Central and Eastern Europe: Macroeconomic Effects on Western Countries*. (April 1992)
187. Michele Fratianni, Jürgen von Hagen, and Christopher Waller, *The Maastricht Way to EMU*. (June 1992)
188. Pierre-Richard Agénor, *Parallel Currency Markets in Developing Countries: Theory, Evidence, and Policy Implications*. (November 1992)
189. Beatriz Armendariz de Aghion and John Williamson, *The G-7's Joint-and-Several Blunder*. (April 1993)
190. Paul Krugman, *What Do We Need to Know about the International Monetary System?* (July 1993)
191. Peter M. Garber and Michael G. Spencer, *The Dissolution of the Austro-Hungarian Empire: Lessons for Currency Reform*. (February 1994)
192. Raymond F. Mikesell, *The Bretton Woods Debates: A Memoir*. (March 1994)
193. Graham Bird, *Economic Assistance to Low-Income Countries: Should the Link be Resurrected?* (July 1994)
194. Lorenzo Bini-Smaghi, Tommaso Padoa-Schioppa, and Francesco Papadia, *The Transition to EMU in the Maastricht Treaty*. (November 1994)
195. Ariel Buira, *Reflections on the International Monetary System*. (January 1995)
196. Shinji Takagi, *From Recipient to Donor: Japan's Official Aid Flows, 1945 to 1990 and Beyond*. (March 1995)
197. Patrick Conway, *Currency Proliferation: The Monetary Legacy of the Soviet Union*. (June 1995)
198. Barry Eichengreen, *A More Perfect Union? The Logic of Economic Integration*. (June 1996)
199. Peter B. Kenen, ed., with John Arrowsmith, Paul De Grauwe, Charles A. E. Goodhart, Daniel Gros, Luigi Spaventa, and Niels Thygesen, *Making EMU Happen—Problems and Proposals: A Symposium*. (August 1996)
200. Peter B. Kenen, ed., with Lawrence H. Summers, William R. Cline, Barry Eichengreen, Richard Portes, Arminio Fraga, and Morris Goldstein, *From Halifax to Lyons: What Has Been Done about Crisis Management?* (October 1996)
201. Louis W. Pauly, *The League of Nations and the Foreshadowing of the International Monetary Fund*. (December 1996)
202. Harold James, *Monetary and Fiscal Unification in Nineteenth-Century Germany: What Can Kohl Learn from Bismarck?* (March 1997)
203. Andrew Crockett, *The Theory and Practice of Financial Stability*. (April 1997)
204. Benjamin J. Cohen, *The Financial Support Fund of the OECD: A Failed Initiative*. (June 1997)

205. Robert N. McCauley, *The Euro and the Dollar*. (November 1997)
206. Thomas Laubach and Adam S. Posen, *Disciplined Discretion: Monetary Targeting in Germany and Switzerland*. (December 1997)
207. Stanley Fischer, Richard N. Cooper, Rudiger Dornbusch, Peter M. Garber, Carlos Massad, Jacques J. Polak, Dani Rodrik, and Savak S. Tarapore, *Should the IMF Pursue Capital-Account Convertibility?* (May 1998)
208. Charles P. Kindleberger, *Economic and Financial Crises and Transformations in Sixteenth-Century Europe*. (June 1998)
209. Maurice Obstfeld, *EMU: Ready or Not?* (July 1998)
210. Wilfred Ethier, *The International Commercial System*. (September 1998)
211. John Williamson and Molly Mahar, *A Survey of Financial Liberalization*. (November 1998)
212. Ariel Buira, *An Alternative Approach to Financial Crises*. (February 1999)
213. Barry Eichengreen, Paul Masson, Miguel Savastano, and Sunil Sharma, *Transition Strategies and Nominal Anchors on the Road to Greater Exchange-Rate Flexibility*. (April 1999)
214. Curzio Giannini, *"Enemy of None but a Common Friend of All"? An International Perspective on the Lender-of-Last-Resort Function*. (June 1999)
215. Jeffrey A. Frankel, *No Single Currency Regime Is Right for All Countries or at All Times*. (August 1999)
216. Jacques J. Polak, *Streamlining the Financial Structure of the International Monetary Fund*. (September 1999)
217. Gustavo H. B. Franco, *The Real Plan and the Exchange Rate*. (April 2000)
218. Thomas D. Willett, *International Financial Markets as Sources of Crises or Discipline: The Too Much, Too Late Hypothesis*. (May 2000)
219. Richard H. Clarida, *G-3 Exchange-Rate Relationships: A Review of the Record and of Proposals for Change*. (September 2000)
220. Stanley Fischer, *On the Need for an International Lender of Last Resort*. (November 2000)
221. Benjamin J. Cohen, *Life at the Top: International Currencies in the Twenty-First Century*. (December 2000)
222. Akihiro Kanaya and David Woo, *The Japanese Banking Crisis of the 1990s: Sources and Lessons*. (June 2001)
223. Yung Chul Park, *The East Asian Dilemma: Restructuring Out or Growing Out?* (August 2001)
224. Felipe Larrain B. and Andrés Velasco, *Exchange-Rate Policy in Emerging-Market Economies*. (December 2001)
225. T. N. Srinivasan, *Trade, Development, and Growth*. (December 2001)
226. Graham Bird and Ramkishen S. Rajan, *The Evolving Asian Financial Architecture*. (February 2002)

PRINCETON STUDIES IN INTERNATIONAL ECONOMICS
(formerly Princeton Studies in International Finance)

72. George M. von Furstenberg and Joseph P. Daniels, *Economic Summit Declarations, 1975-1989: Examining the Written Record of International Cooperation*. (February 1992)

73. Ishac Diwan and Dani Rodrik, *External Debt, Adjustment, and Burden Sharing: A Unified Framework.* (November 1992)
74. Barry Eichengreen, *Should the Maastricht Treaty Be Saved?* (December 1992)
75. Adam Klug, *The German Buybacks, 1932-1939: A Cure for Overhang?* (November 1993)
76. Tamim Bayoumi and Barry Eichengreen, *One Money or Many? Analyzing the Prospects for Monetary Unification in Various Parts of the World.* (September 1994)
77. Edward E. Leamer, *The Heckscher-Ohlin Model in Theory and Practice.* (February 1995)
78. Thorvaldur Gylfason, *The Macroeconomics of European Agriculture.* (May 1995)
79. Angus S. Deaton and Ronald I. Miller, *International Commodity Prices, Macroeconomic Performance, and Politics in Sub-Saharan Africa.* (December 1995)
80. Chander Kant, *Foreign Direct Investment and Capital Flight.* (April 1996)
81. Gian Maria Milesi-Ferretti and Assaf Razin, *Current-Account Sustainability.* (October 1996)
82. Pierre-Richard Agénor, *Capital-Market Imperfections and the Macroeconomic Dynamics of Small Indebted Economies.* (June 1997)
83. Michael Bowe and James W. Dean, *Has the Market Solved the Sovereign-Debt Crisis?* (August 1997)
84. Willem H. Buiter, Giancarlo M. Corsetti, and Paolo A. Pesenti, *Interpreting the ERM Crisis: Country-Specific and Systemic Issues.* (March 1998)
85. Holger C. Wolf, *Transition Strategies: Choices and Outcomes.* (June 1999)
86. Alessandro Prati and Garry J. Schinasi, *Financial Stability in European Economic and Monetary Union.* (August 1999)
87. Peter Hooper, Karen Johnson, and Jaime Marquez, *Trade Elasticities for the G-7 Countries.* (August 2000)
88. Ramkishen S. Rajan, *(Ir)relevance of Currency-Crisis Theory to the Devaluation and Collapse of the Thai Baht.* (February 2001)
89. Lucio Sarno and Mark P. Taylor, *The Microstructure of the Foreign-Exchange Market: A Selective Survey of the Literature.* (May 2001)

SPECIAL PAPERS IN INTERNATIONAL ECONOMICS

17. Richard Pomfret, *International Trade Policy with Imperfect Competition.* (August 1992)
18. Hali J. Edison, *The Effectiveness of Central-Bank Intervention: A Survey of the Literature After 1982.* (July 1993)
19. Sylvester W.C. Eijffinger and Jakob De Haan, *The Political Economy of Central-Bank Independence.* (May 1996)
20. Olivier Jeanne, *Currency Crises: A Perspective on Recent Theoretical Developments.* (March 2000)

REPRINTS IN INTERNATIONAL FINANCE

29. Peter B. Kenen, *Sorting Out Some EMU Issues*; reprinted from Jean Monnet Chair Paper 38, Robert Schuman Centre, European University Institute, 1996. (December 1996)

fold over, seal, and send

∘ SUBSCRIBE ∘ ORDER ∘

INTERNATIONAL ECONOMICS SECTION

SUBSCRIPTIONS

Rate $45 a year

The International Economics Section issues six to eight publications each year in a mix of Essays and Studies. Late subscribers receive all publications for the subscription year. Prepayment is required and may be made by check in U.S. dollars or by Visa or MasterCard. A complete list of publications (including previously issued Special Papers and Reprints) is available at www.princeton.edu/~ies.

Address inquiries to:

International Economics Section
Department of Economics, Fisher Hall
Princeton University
Princeton, NJ 08544–1021

BOOK ORDERS

Essays, Studies, Special Papers
& Reprints $10.00

plus postage

Within U.S. $1.50
Outside U.S. (surface mail) $4.00

_____

Discounts are available for
orders of five or more publications.

_____

Telephone: 609–258–4048
Telefax: 609–258–1374
E-mail: ies@princeton.edu

fold up

INTERNATIONAL ECONOMICS SECTION

This is a subscription ☐ ; a book order ☐

Essay #(s) _____, _____ No. of copies___

Study #(s) _____, _____ No. of copies___

Special Paper # _____ No. of copies ___

Reprint # _____ No. of copies ___

☐ Enclosed is my check made payable to Princeton University, International Economics Section

totaling $_____.

Please charge: ☐ Visa ☐ MasterCard

Acct.# _____

Expires _____

Signature_____

Send to:

Name_____

Address_____

City _____

State _____Zip _____

Country_____

INTERNATIONAL ECONOMICS SECTION
DEPARTMENT OF ECONOMICS
FISHER HALL
PRINCETON UNIVERSITY
PRINCETON, NJ 08544-1021